RELATE

Unlocking the Power of the Six Personality Types to Strengthen Your Relationships

CHARLES CAUSEY

"In this masterful **exposé** on contemporary human experience, Charles Causey tackles one of the most debilitating emotional/spiritual plagues assailing mankind today, namely, loneliness. With our modern access to advanced communications media, one would reasonably predict improved human connection in both quantity and quality. But this has proven decidedly untrue. Indeed, the opposite seems to be happening. Charles takes this unfortunate reality to task and offers up his *RELATE* model as a viable means of grappling with loneliness and setting oneself on course for personal/relational fulfillment. This book is at once thought-provoking and practical—grounded and groundbreaking. It is a must read for anyone who has had, is currently enduring, or ever expects to suffer relational discord. In other words, it is a book for everyone!"

-Dr. Mark A. Tinsley
College Professor, Pastor, and Army Chaplain

"Relationships are always messy. It's the very nature of humanity, and then every once in a while, there is a tool that comes along to help bring clarity on how we can better show up in those relationships. Charles has done that with *RELATE*. The tool is profound in the way it calls out our inner being and illustrates how we show up with the people we care about the most. I can't wait to see how relationships grow through the use of this practical and important writing."

-Rev. Tony Miltenberger
Podcast host of the Reclamation Podcast, CEO and Founder of
Follow-to-Lead Coaching

RELATE

Unlocking the Power of Personality Types to Strengthen Your Relationships

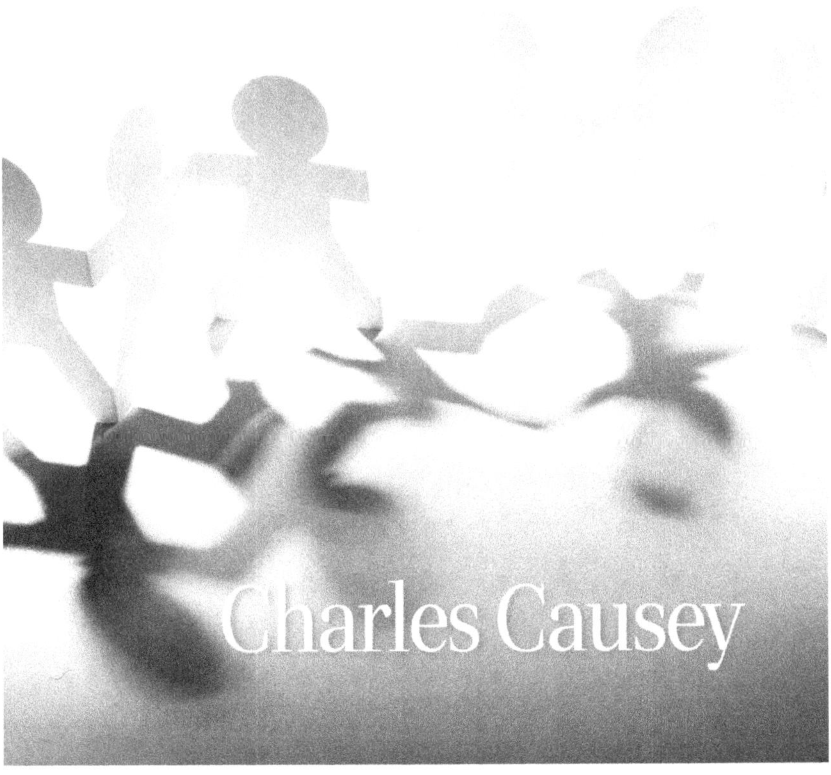

Charles Causey

*Edited by
Vicki Zimmer*

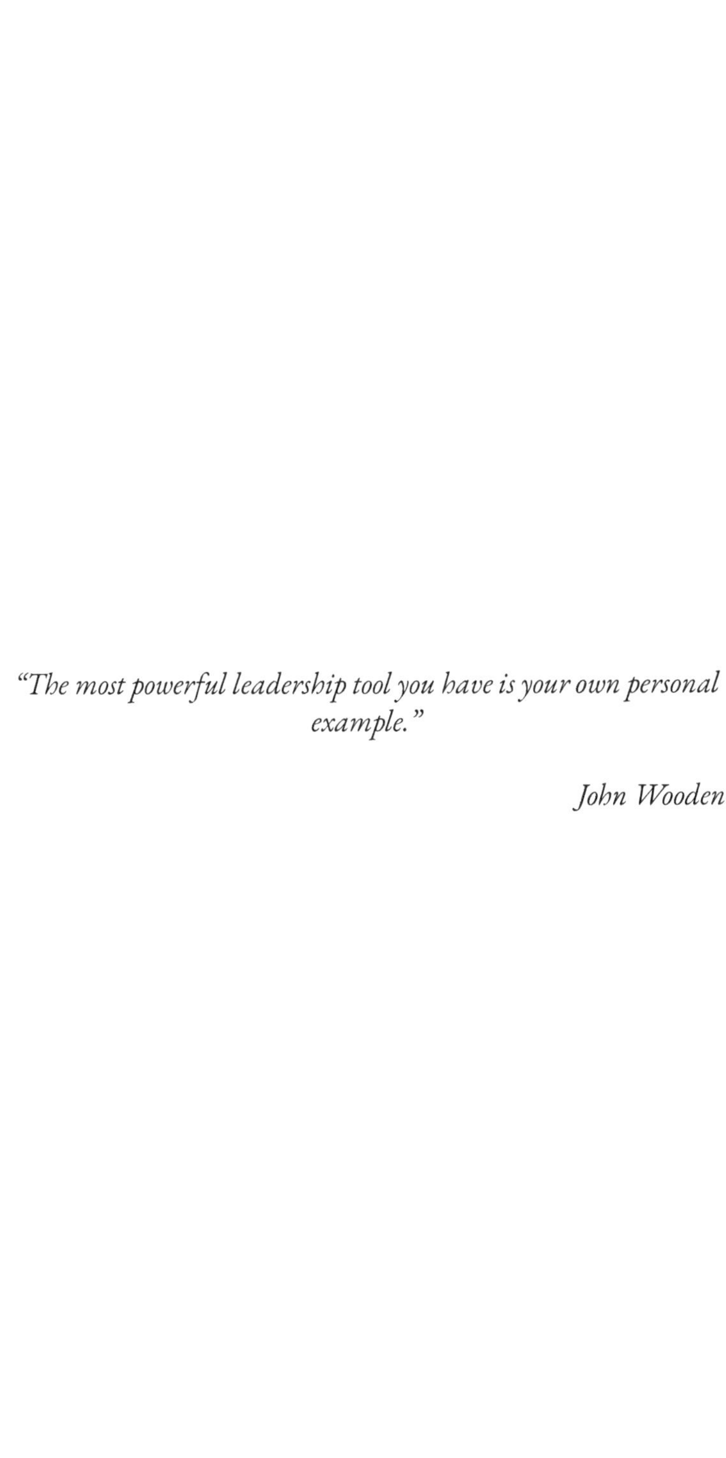

"The most powerful leadership tool you have is your own personal example."

John Wooden

CONTENTS

THE IMPORTANCE OF RELATIONSHIPS

In 1938, researchers at Harvard University embarked on an eighty-year study to find out what makes people happy in life. For decades, they worked with participants from all over the world by asking them detailed questions at two-year intervals. The answers they found were somewhat surprising. It was not money, career achievement, power, fame, or fitness and beauty that made people happy. It was something simpler; something everyone has the opportunity to achieve no matter what you look like, or how much money you make. The answer is ... positive relationships. More than money and fame, close relationships are what keep people happy throughout their lives.

This answer is so intuitive and seemingly knowable and appreciated by all, it almost makes you laugh at Harvard for not comprehending this without a study. Yet it is not as common as one might think. Obviously, without having to look too far, it is easy to encounter a lot of people from broken homes, damaged relationships, and broken hearts. It is clear that closeness with others is a good thing and should be pursued, but many struggle to make it a reality and, unfortunately, even though deep personal friendships is the longing of their soul, their actions push others away. Plus, with technology that is supposed to expand access to friendships, it sometimes keeps us from establishing deep and meaningful relationships. The latest health news contains articles about loneliness being on the rise, even among adolescents, and I heard on the radio yesterday, from the Centers for Disease Control and Prevention (CDC), that young women are battling record levels of violence, sadness, and suicide risk. In the last five years, hopelessness has increased from 36 percent to 57 percent in this demographic. Sadly, this means a majority of young women are not on the path of happiness.

So, the great human dilemma is, *how do I develop close and long-lasting relationships?* That question is the impetus for this book. I believe I have a message of hope for those pursuing a deeper sense of contentment and joy. I have personally been blessed with many close relationships from all walks of life, race, religion, and nationality. My profession allowed me the opportunity to travel the world and work with people from many diverse backgrounds. Whether I was taking a boat expedition down a distributary of a central African waterway to work with one of the most remote tribes in the world, or meeting with national leaders or high school students on islands in the South Pacific, I can affirm that healthy, wholesome relationships are the foundation of every civilization. From Tonga to East Timor, and from Japan to The Netherlands, the families I met and the friendships I forged around the world illuminated what makes a life that is joyful, abundant, and full of purpose; chiefly one built on dynamic, healthy relationships. For what it's worth, this book you are holding is a fountain, an outpouring to bring greater contentment and joy for people in relationships. My hope is that it will help people forge an enduring closeness with teammates, friends, and family in ways they never thought possible.

WHO AM I?

THE THEORY BEHIND EVERYTHING

Who am I? This seemingly odd question has been asked by many people, maybe even you. The quest to understand human personality has been one of the great studies of scientists and philosophers for thousands of years. A little focus on one's identity from time to time does not mean one is too self-focused; on the contrary, it can be helpful to become more understanding of others in deeper and more meaningful ways. In fact, it can help you become more relatable and make close friends.

So, who are you? Have you personally thought about it? Are you easy to get to know and easy to get along with? Or do you struggle at making close friends, or finding people with similar interests? Are you self-absorbed and lack empathy? Would anyone tell you if that is true, and would you believe them? Do other people mostly bore you? Do you try to be the life of the party? These are intriguing questions to ask, but when you think about the answers it often takes more than a little self-reflection. Some might say they are somewhere in the middle, or that it depends on who they are with at the time. Which brings up an interesting point—frame of reference.

Albert Einstein's theory of special relativity was instrumental to show that all motion must be relative to a frame of reference. It discusses how speed affects mass, time, and space. For instance, imagine two people playing ping pong on a train that is moving forty miles per hour. To them, the ball they are hitting is traveling at one speed, but to someone not on the train, the ball they are hitting is moving at a completely different speed—the speed of the train plus the speed of the ball. As Einstein points out in his theory (using various analogies), all motion is relative, and the measurement of motion depends on the position of the observer.

When considering Einstein's theory as a backdrop to personality types, the measurement or description of someone's personality depends partially on the frame of reference of the observer. Personality types can be distinct, but they are somewhat relative depending on with which type they are interacting with at the time, and in what setting. It is a truism that some people act differently when they encounter certain personality types or encounter different settings. This will be considered more throughout the book, but for now it is important to consider how personalities can morph and change depending on the interaction. And if someone is suffering from neuroticism or narcissism it can skew their perspective.

So what kind of personalities are there? There is a difference between a personality trait and a personality type. In our contemporary times, scientists acknowledge a taxonomy, or classification system, of five personality traits called the Big-5 or the Five Factor model. The five traits are: openness, conscientiousness, extraversion, agreeableness, and neuroticism. Most personality psychologists believe these five dimensions are universal, psychometrically sound, and have predictive validity. In essence, the scientific community seems convinced that these five traits are displayed by every person on a spectrum from low to high. Studies working with hundreds of thousands of people have given those in the field of psychology an assurance that the five traits can be utilized as a framework in which to look more deeply into personality.

The study of personality *types* is a much more elusive endeavor than looking at traits. It is easy to see that someone might be more conscientious than another; meaning that they are more diligent, careful, and thoughtful. Or that someone might be more neurotic, meaning that they possess a disposition of negative emotions like anxiety, anger, or irritability. But to put the varying degree of traits into a cluster and call it a personality type involves more careful consideration. Some of the most popular groupings in our society are the DISC model with its four types, the Myers-Briggs Type Indicator with its sixteen types, and the Enneagram model of typology with its nine types. In my own estimation, working with thousands of people over thirty years, though informative, I've found these personality models somewhat clunky for reasons I will outline below. In vain did I search for a more perfect assessment tool. So I finally developed one from my own research and understanding of human psychology.

As a counselor and relationship coach, I assist in helping people understand their own personality, and provide them pathways to develop healthy relationships with others. In this work, I needed a tool which accounted for some of the main ways people interact with their world. For instance, one extremely important defining characteristic I have observed in distinguishing personalities (that has contributed to many inter-personal arguments) is how some individuals are socially coop erative in their decision-making; which means they like to adhere to societies' prescribed methods of functioning. Other people are utilitarian in their decision-making; which means they possess a positive attitude toward those things that are productive and efficient, and possess a negative attitude toward those things that are ineffective and useless. (*For a detailed*

For example, the socially cooperative person will not go down a road the wrong way for twenty yards, even if it means driving an extra two miles around in a circle to get back to roughly the same point. *There is a sign there for a reason!* Many might think, yeah, it's good not to break the law. However, what if it was in a rural setting, at two in the morning, with no other vehicles in sight? Many individuals, especially the utilitarian personality, would consider this as easy justification for going the wrong way. Another road example would be if traffic was merging into the left lane because a mile ahead the right lane is closed. A socially cooperative personality type would seek to merge as soon as possible so they have peace of mind and do not cause a headache for others down the road. A utilitarian personality type would like to see how far down the right lane they can go before having to merge. In fact, they would argue that it helps traffic flow to do this.

Life is made up of many decisions like these, and people are typically on one side of the coin or the other; either socially cooperative or utilitarian. How much driver angst is caused by a co-passenger having a divergent personality type? This is merely one example. I have discovered other defining characteristics as well, such as if people are abstract thinkers or concrete thinkers, or to what degree they are individualistic, intuitive, and idealistic. More will be shared on these items later.

So to bring home these points and going back to who you are, are you mostly agreeable to others? Are you conscientious? Do you possess a great deal of neuroticism? In an honest assessment, we all know people who seem irritable, no matter when you might be around them. Others seem agreeable, nearly all the time. Other questions that could be asked are: What makes people more resilient? What makes people controlling? What keeps some people extremely closed off to candid feedback and others more open? Or, one of the most interesting questions, what makes some people seem so humble?

As mentioned previously, in the span of over thirty years, I have counseled thousands of individuals and personality tested many of them. This testing typically included post-analysis counseling with them or was used during life-success and marriage conferences or in conjunction with professional training for vocational counselors and military leaders. My research found that the major personality traits can be summed up into six distinct personality types. (*Please refer to the Endnotes for more information on RELATE provenance.*) These six types are ubiquitous with what we see in the world and will be very hard *not to* see them once you are exposed to them.

Before discussing the nuances of each of the six types (in Chapters 2-7), I want to do two things: First, introduce the benefits of the *RELATE* personality model, since it is categorically newer than any other model. And second, briefly introduce the distinctions between the two supergroup categories, the Executives and the Explorers.

THE BENEFITS OF THE *RELATE* MODEL

First off, one benefit of *RELATE*, which is also an acronym for the six personality types, is that it doesn't focus extensively on extroversion and introversion. In my opinion, this clustering can be a distraction from the core elements of one's being. Typically, society has either uplifted extroversion or condemned it. But in my study, it is an unnecessary characterization, except in the degree that some people remain closed off and reserved to the point of not wanting to change. For instance, I've noticed some extroverts can monologue on any number of topics, except peering into their own soul and being vulnerable ... "Hey, now you're getting a little too personal!" Whereas some supposed introverts, who do not speak out as freely, can be very open to share their inner feelings and struggles with inadequacy. So, who is the extrovert in this case?

Another factor surfacing in my research revealed there is a vast swath of people who are neither especially extroverted nor introverted; they are somewhere in the middle. Using a scale of one to ten, with a one being a strong introvert and a ten being a high extrovert, how are we to categorize those who score between four and six? What I have found is that not only is this a worthy category of people to acknowledge, but a large percentage of people fall into this middle territory; perhaps up to 40 percent of the population! This is one of the areas where I think our personality-testing forefathers did us a disservice. These "middle people," for a lack of a better term, are more extroverted in some settings, and in other settings display traits of introversion; perhaps when they are stressed or have a big project to complete or are in a setting where there is discord. Don't we all know people who are extroverts around good friends and family but introverts around people they do not know very well, or in public? This is a group that must be accounted for in order to explore the full dynamic of personality. We can't just leave out 40 percent of the population, or force them into boxes that don't adequately describe them.

As you can see, there are multiple issues plaguing the distinction between extroverts and introverts. Therefore, with my six types, those people in the middle are described in the main; meaning, I focus on the middle folks. I occasionally add brief commentary on how these people might act if they are more introverted or extroverted. This is a very unique factor in the *RELATE* model. So, to clarify, there are indeed only six major arteries of personality, from which each type can be varied by the degree of introversion, middlemost, or extroversion as part of their personality. But I leave it for the

> *There is a vast swath of people who are neither especially extroverted or introverted!*

individual reader to interpolate how their personality type embodies their specific degree of outgoingness.

Another strength of this model is the fact that it is only six types as compared to sixteen or more with other personality tests. It can be a struggle for most people to comprehend the complexities of more than a dozen personality types, especially those types we seldom, if ever, see in society. I have happily discovered that over 99 percent of individuals tested were able to identify closely to one of the six *RELATE* types. It is another one of my theories that having too many types is a burdensome red-herring for people who are simply looking to identify truths about themselves and shore up some blind spots. Having fewer types is an efficient tool in order to remember what makes each type distinct.

I also discovered that personality models are not specific enough to have only four or five types. My theory is that what we call "personality" chiefly manifests itself into six distinct types in humanity, and people will easily find themselves within one of these types. One of my six personality types has a modification that creates a sub-type. Using a solar system analogy, some of the material of the planet is separate or unique enough to distinguish it from the planet proper, so it could be considered a moon, but it is not a unique planet. Overall, I found that four or five types were too few, and that eight or more types were too many. Life experience, along with research and testing, revealed that within these six (and a half) types, people can adequately identify themselves and those around them. My hope is that readers will find this to be an extremely effective personality tool and will be a source to bring greater health to relationships, especially by those who've found previous personality models unsatisfying.

> **The major personality traits can be summed up into six distinct personality types!**

In conclusion, what I have streamlined in this method is not present in other models. *RELATE* is not overly focused on vocational targeting; its focus is in developing healthy, wholesome relationships, which, as we know from the Harvard study, brings the most joy in life. And with only six types, it not only facilitates finding your unique type, but it is also easy to remember all the types. Intentionally, the technique to simplify this model is that the six types can be found in an acronym using the first letter for each type. The word by which to remember this model is the title of this book, *RELATE*. *RELATE* stands for the words:

Role Model
Energizer
Loyalist
Assertive
Trailblazer
Expressive

The words above represent the six personality types. The words of each type are not empty labels, they are descriptors that get right to the heart of each personality type. As mentioned before, it is only the Loyalist type that has a sub-type attached to it (described in Chapter 4).

In my initial observations, I found that three of these types represented similar patterns in how they participate in the world and in what is important to them. The Role Models, Loyalists, and Assertives make up the family, or supergroup, called **Executives**; this is because they respond similarly in how they use power, how they handle difficulty, and how they process data. Similarly, I refer to the Energizers, Trailblazers, and Expressives with the term **Explorers**; this is because of how they see the world and how they approach the unknown. These two collections of personality types, the Executives and the Explorers, comprise the *RELATE* ensemble, just as the National Football

League is comprised of the American Football Conference and the National Football Conference. However, as described above, with extended research and study I found that I needed to insert one caveat, which accords this model more precision.

I discovered that with the Loyalist group, the majority of them (75 percent) fall into the Executive category, but there is a sub-type minority (25 percent) that falls into the Explorer category. This is the only personality type which straddles both the Executive and Explorer families. For clarity, I call the Executive Loyalists by the sole term Loyalists and the Explorer Loyalists using both words.

EXECUTIVES VS EXPLORERS

In order to deepen your familiarity of the *RELATE* model, here is a snapshot of the distinctions between Executives (Role Models, Loyalists, and Assertives) and Explorers (Energizers, Trailblazers, Expressives, and Explorer Loyalists) in the following diagram.

Family

EXECUTIVE | ROLE MODEL | LOYALIST | ASSERTIVE

Family

EXPLORER | ENERGIZER | TRAILBLAZER | EXPRESSIVE | EXPLORER LOYALIST

KEY EXECUTIVE TRAITS
* Loves structure
* More black and white vs gray and hazy
* What you see is what you get
* Focus on making decisions
* Ruled by deadlines
* Makes lists and uses them
* Easy to focus on the goal
* More authoritarian with power
* Institutional guidelines are important
* Tends to like what is practical
* Likes to get things planned and ready
* Seeks closure
* People in error should be punished
* Wants to be seen as reasonable
* Likes to see how things have worked in the past

KEY EXPLORER TRAITS
* Loves understanding others
* Adapts easily with new info
* Work can also be play
* Stimulated by deadlines
* Makes lists to organize thoughts
* Loves to be spontaneous
* More diplomatic with power
* Tries to negotiate before punishing
* Rarely focus on negative outcomes
* Uses relationship finesse as power
* Is open-minded as long as possible
* Loves to generate alternatives
* Gives plenty of benefit of the doubt
* Wants to be seen as spontaneous
* Likes to consider unusual facts and scenarios

To dig a little deeper, and to see the difference between Executives and Explorers portrayed in the three categories of power, handling difficulty and processing data, please refer to the Endnotes in the final pages of the book. With these thoughts as a preface, it is time to familiarize you with the six personality types. You are encouraged to complete a forty-eight-question assessment tool online which will automatically score your results and give you your personality type. The website is *www.sixpersonalities.com*. When you've received your assessment results, please continue reading the following six chapters which will explain the six personality types. I can't wait for you to discover more about who you are!

A side note: It is understood that one test or assessment can never truly define an individual, so the next few chapters are offered delicately, with respect and appreciation for the complexities of life. Each person is made up of experiences which forge them into unique individuals. Past victories, past trauma, past trials, and time invested overcoming challenges all contribute toward the way each person thinks and acts. We cannot put a label on anyone to determine what they are about. Every day is a gift, and we are often surprised at what life brings us through interactions with other people. What this study does propose is that generally—in a macro sense—each individual usually functions by having preferences and inclinations that flow into one of six channels. The following chapters are offered to bring a sense of joy and freedom, not to restrict or reduce.

ROLE MODEL

Family

Type

EXECUTIVE

ROLE MODEL

LOYALIST

ASSERTIVE

I would like to introduce you to the Role Models. Who are these wonderful people and why are they referred to as Role Models? Role Models always seem like they have their life together and know what should be done. They are responsible and sensible, enjoying what life throws at them. These harmonious people love to help others, usually adding a healthy dose of realism and practicality in their advice. Conscientious and dependable, they work in jobs that are considered the backbone of civilization. They typically like going to work, being around other people, and contributing in a positive way to society. A person is blessed to have a Role Model as a neighbor because they can be counted on to get the mail or feed a pet when needed without forgetting. A Role Model's worst fear is to let down someone who is counting on them.

Role Models make to-do lists and use them. For these responsible types, not only does it feel good to accomplish numerous items each day, they have the tenacity to stick to one task as long as it takes, even if boring. They have a good grasp on what they want in life and believe that accomplishing their established goals is what will help them feel successful. They love to belong to meaningful institutions and don't mind following orders from their superiors. They are dutiful foot soldiers who make great leaders when given the opportunity. Role Models are goal-oriented negotiators who look at the past as a way forward; meaning, if it worked last time why change it? They love the tried and true and flourish when roles are clearly defined, and everyone works hard so that the team accomplishes something great for the organization.

Friendly and sympathetic, Role Models have a strong need to please others. Generous and loyal, is it any wonder why Role Models are a cherished member of a team? They are good, grounded people and believe that others should be good as well. When expectations of others let them down, they can roll with the punches until they feel personally attacked. If feeling misunderstood or betrayed, they can tend to take things personally and become emotional. Down to earth and practical, duties and obligations come before recreation and fun. The true test of a Role Model is that when life doesn't go well for them, they still continue on, trying hard to keep a positive attitude.

Role Models typically speak with great conviction and use the word "should" a lot. One of their greatest fears is letting down someone important to them because they like to be seen as trustworthy, gracious, and thoughtful. They are tied with Loyalists as the most harmonizing of the six personality types; not that the other types struggle with getting along, it's just that for Role Models it is imperative. As their name suggests, they put pressure on themselves to be an example to others and not to disappoint. Their animal is the eagle, flying high as a model for others to see and emulate. Role Models have a lot of noble qualities making them an inspiration to other people. (*A soft warning here, I am not saying the Role Model is the best personality type and should be pursued. The term Role Model is utilized chiefly because these conscientious people aspire to be a good example to others. There is not one personality type better than the others.*)

Some of the things that annoy Role Models is change for change's sake. They must be convinced that a change is important and needed at that moment. Moving to a new town or trying to adapt to a new roommate, who may not be as courteous, can be extremely challenging for them. As a member of the Executive family, Role Models can be seen as strict authoritarians at times and confrontational, perhaps challenging someone with whom they disagree. When people don't respond the way Role Models imagine they should, then they should be punished. The sooner the punishment is over, the faster they can become harmonious again. If the Role Model is the person who committed the wrong then extreme worthlessness and inner guilt is on the way for this type. Their faces usually reflect an accurate description of their feelings.

In order to persuade a Role Model, others must be personal, with uncomplicated rationale. Keeping things practical and positive, it is best to lead by example; show a Role Model how it is done and if it makes sense, the Role Model will readily work it into their routine. It is imperative to respect their feelings, and not try to talk them out of feeling a certain way. Though generally good-humored, most of the time they do not always respond well when they find themselves the butt of a joke or are teased. Of course, this is hard for everyone, but Role Models take umbrage because they usually would not tease others to the point of embarrassment. Role Models go to great lengths to treat people with respect and like it when they are treated in kind. If appreciated, this friendly, giving, and hard-working type will do just about anything for you.

Reliable and big-hearted, I can't emphasize enough how much Role Models crave to experience life with others and use these shared experiences to reminisce and talk about it with others for years. As mentioned in the paragraph above, the only thing that really gets to them is when they feel mistreated, especially in a public setting. One of the potential weaknesses of Role Models is a preoccupation with social status. They crave to be in a position to influence others, and if they feel they are being "knocked down" the social ladder it can be really hard for them. Role Models have definite views of right and wrong. When others are not following through on their commitments or breaking another inviolable rule for the Role Model, then it is hard for the Role Model not to judge them. Also, because Role Models do so many things right and seemingly have a knack for knowing what things are good and worthy to focus on and what things are not, they can get extremely defensive when someone disagrees with them. It is hard for Role Models to accept people who willfully go down the wrong road.

One last note, Role Models are considered concrete, cooperative, and at times even perfectionists. The characteristic that requires more explaining is what concrete means. To be a concrete thinker is to focus on the physical world around you and to take things literally; it is the opposite of being an abstract thinker. No one is totally concrete, and everyone is on a spectrum in how their thinking works. Concrete thinkers tend to take things at face value and are very literal with their words and ideas. They do not read too much into things nor coordinate data to come up with alternative or imaginary meanings. Children are typically more concrete in their thinking, believing what they see and trusting the words they hear. This doesn't mean the Role Model is naïve. On the contrary, it means they are judicious and generous, always ready to give a fair hearing to others. For instance, when dealing with a new group of people, Role Models are somewhat trusting of others until they get burned by them; then their excellent memories use caution when dealing with those who have mistreated them in the past. Skilled in diplomacy, Role Models adhere to the ancient proverb that "A hot-tempered person stirs up strife but one who is slow to anger quiets contention."

Here is how two different Role Models describe their lives:

Sophie says: *I like being a Role Model because it is nice to have some influence on other people, especially when I know I'm right. One thing that's true, that others may not know about me or have a wrong idea about me, is that I'm self-conscious, not self-confident in most areas. And I always think that people think that as a Role Model I can just do it, and I will do it. But as I've gotten older, I struggle with being sure that I can do it because you don't want to disappoint anyone ever, and because you feel like people are counting on you. I get frustrated in a group setting when someone doesn't pull their weight. I don't want someone to get credit when they don't deserve it. For the people who really care and work hard and do well, it's frustrating when there are* *laggers back there who get the same credit. The best way to motivate me is when I'm in a time crunch, then I have to get it done. This is true for me because I'm a little bit of a procrastinator. When people are counting on me and I have to get it done, then that motivates me. I feel better being a worker bee instead of being in charge because then I know what my job is and what needs to be done. Somebody else can tell me what needs to be done and I can take it from there, but I don't want to decide everything that needs to be done. A pet peeve of mine is inconsiderateness, especially when someone is not being nice to another person. An instance of this is like in a store, when a parent is cussing at a child, or someone speaking really down on others. A big rule for me is to be nice and kind to others.*

Clayton says: *I love the Role Model type; if everyone was this type, how wonderful the world could be. Everything would be well-ordered, like with a group project, it works best when everyone knows their role and how they can contribute best toward the end goal. A lot would get done; you know what you want and then you go to achieve it and still be able to have fun while you're doing it. I do well in genuine crisis and real stress. I think I do worse in manufactured crises. At the end of the day, I am going to get it done and do what it takes. In real situations I am calm and reasonable. What others may not realize is that I am very flexible and open-minded. Some might see me as more stiff, put together, and efficient, but more than they might realize, I am flexible and not as rigid as I appear to be. One thing that bugs me at work is when people get sloppy and try to cut corners or don't try. Just do your best and at least try. Part of that is in the profession I am in, where we have to do the right thing and can't cut corners. Also, when people are mean and domineering, that is always frustrating. It is possible to do things kindly. In almost all situations being kind and polite is an option. In a group setting, when people are indecisive and no one is willing to take charge, that is frustrating. I* *don't want to trample on people, but I think someone needs to speak up and figure it out. That gets down to the idea that things work better when everyone knows their role and how they can best contribute. The best way to motivate me is to show me the end result of what the outcome can be. What is the expected outcome? If it is a good thing, then let's go, I'll do whatever it takes to get there. I feel better being in charge than being a worker bee because it is the best use of my talents and abilities. It gives more independence, and you can become your full best self and leverage your good qualities to help the entire team. And there is a harmonious aspect there too, where you can have some control and set the tone for the group dynamic. A pet peeve of mine is when people don't listen, and people don't care about big things and small things. People should use their talents and gifts to do something great. And especially if it is something I care about, I want people to care and be invested with me and choose something good. I don't want to control and force others; I want people to come to a shared vision, and for people to know why I want to do something and agree with me on that.*

It is obvious from these two contributions that it is really annoying for Role Models when they see someone putting another person down, or not pulling their weight. Since Role Models are usually respectful and courteous to those around them, they expect others to operate that way as well. For other types reading these paragraphs, take note that belittling someone else in front of a Role Model will get you in their crosshairs.

For each personality, I will highlight four lead traits which go to the heart of their character and present an easy-to-read tool which summarizes that type so the reader can see a snapshot to assist with understanding these people. This will be followed by a list of strengths, blind spots, and methods to shine and grow.

The four lead traits of Role Models are: (1) *Responsible*, which means they love to contribute when needed and are answerable and accountable; (2) *Trusting*, which means they are generous with their faith and inclined to believe what others say; (3) *Considerate*, which means they are careful not to inconvenience others; and (4) *Cooperative*, which means they are eager to please and usually agreeable.

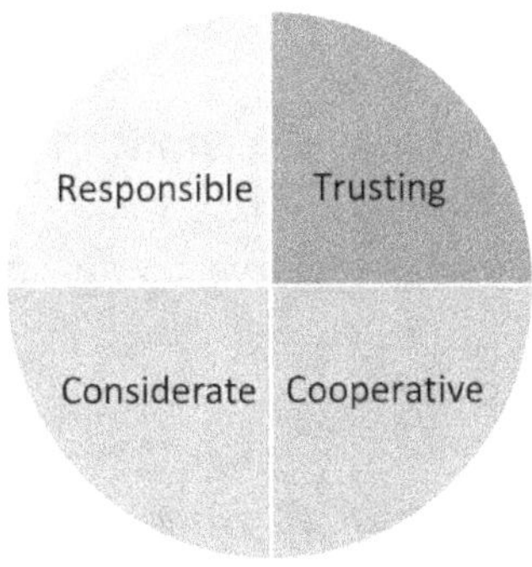

Here is a snapshot of the Role Model type:

Type: *Role Model*

Family: *Executive*

Hallmark: *Responsible People*

Predominate Goal with Others: *Eager to help others*

Sayings Attractive to Role Models: *What can I do for you? What's the right thing to do? A friend in need is a friend indeed! I really appreciate your help.*

Quest 1: *Belonging*

Quest 2: *To feel valued*

With a dash of: *Self-doubt*

Superpower: *Ability to focus on a task or goal until completion*

Achilles heel: *Guilt creator in themselves and others*

Others' perceptions: *Role Models are polite, proper, and engaging people*

Most: *Diplomatic*

Not too much: *Rambunctious*

Worst fears: *Afraid of not being good enough, letting others down, and being abandoned*

Role Models want to be seen as: *Confident*

When Role Models are under great stress: *As stress mounts, Role Models initially exhibit denial and try to bury things with additional "forced" pleasantness. When harmony is jeopardized (though they may question the validity of the discord), Role Models go to great lengths to restore it, such as bringing someone a gift, or taking a sick person chicken noodle soup. With extra stress, their need to control a project or another person skyrockets. They over-personalize and heap guilt onto themselves because they believe that they are a central part of the issue.*

How to win their heart: *Genuinely express your appreciation for them, respect their feelings, and never accuse them of being irrational.*

Famous historical figures who typify the Role Model: *Harry S. Truman, Pope Francis, Colin Powell, Barbara Walters, Sam Walton, Sarah Palin, Whitney Houston, Elton John*

Animal: *Eagle*

<u>Strengths:</u>

- Possess a strong sense of duty

22 Role Model Traits
Exemplar
Responsible
Trusting
Considerate
Cooperative
Dutiful
Appropriate
Enjoys challenges
Polite
Competitive
Purposeful
Settled
Accountable
Tolerant
Diplomatic
Attentive
Steadiness
Persevering
Diligent
Dependable
Consistent
Harmonizing

- Supremely helpful to others
- Ability to stick to a task and work hard
- Excellent team member when working on a project together
- Polite, respectful, and encouraging
- Goal-oriented people helpers
- Extremely harmonious and generous
- Love to have fun once the work is complete
- Loyal and can be relied upon
- Praise and nurture good behavior in others
- Caring people who want to assist those in need
- Great drive and determination to get things accomplished and be productive

<u>Possible Blind Spots:</u>

- Sometimes seen as rigid and opinionated
- Can be too concerned about social status
- Can create guilt in others
- Can work so hard for others they feel taken advantage of
- If confronted with a wrongdoing, extreme worthlessness and martyrdom follow
- A tendency to take on too much of a task themselves, without asking for help
- A reluctance to embrace new and untested ideas
- A tendency to be stubborn or fixed when hearing opposing viewpoints
- Can become overburdened carrying other people's problems
- Seek to avoid conflict at the expense of dealing with issues
- Can make decisions prematurely, before all the useful information is gathered
- Vulnerable to criticism

<u>Ways to Grow and Shine as a Role Model:</u>

- Think more about the future and try to consider possibilities that don't already exist
- When in a new work or volunteer environment ask your supervisor to clarify goals and expectations
- Work at not taking things so personal; consider that others aren't out to get you
- Slow down, ask for help, and create realistic goals
- Don't permanently write off someone who has offended you
- Find people you can trust to give you candid feedback
- Spend less time in activities where there is frequent interpersonal conflict, yet don't withdraw from family or good friends in the process; boundaries are key
- Don't run the risk of making decisions too hastily before all needed data has been analyzed
- Understand your tendency to induce guilt in others, refrain from saying something to specifically make someone else feel bad
- Allow room in your world view to hear another person's point of view, even if it appears ludicrous

<u>A Few Hints When Dealing with Explorers:</u>

When speaking to a member of the Explorer family (Energizers, Trailblazers, and Expressives), remember that they are not out to get you; they are hardwired differently and may at times be confusing to you, but they are not the enemy. Role Models may have an especially hard time with Trailblazers who sometimes say things simply to poke or prod without intentionally meaning to harm someone. Trailblazers sometimes have no idea how sensitive Role Models can be because Role Models usually seem so put together. Expressives will love the opportunity to share with you all about their lives, but Role Models, though gracious and understanding, need to prevent themselves from becoming a dumping ground for other people emotionally. Energizers may wear out Role Models with how they can transition from project to project, seemingly managing everything at once. Energizers' love for action and adventure may become tiresome to the street-smart Role Model. (For a more detailed description of how Role Models interact with other types, see Chapter Nine.)

Write down some names of friends who you suspect might be Role Models:

1. __________________________

2. __________________________

3. __________________________

ENERGIZER

Family   Type

<table>
<tr>
<td>E
X
P
L
O
R
E
R</td>
<td>E
N
E
R
G
I
Z
E
R</td>
<td>T
R
A
I
L
B
L
A
Z
E
R</td>
<td>E
X
P
R
E
S
S
I
V
E</td>
</tr>
</table>

I would like to introduce you to the Energizers. Who are these amazing people and why are they referred to as Energizers? It is true that all the other types have energy and can be high-producing people, yet the reason this buoyant group of people are known as Energizers is because more than any other type, they tend to hop from one thing to the next with gusto. And not just with projects, but with people, activities, things on their to do list, and conversations. Versatile and fun to be around, they usually appear full of boundless energy. Energizers are like people magnets; their smile and laughter draw others to them.

Playful and generous, Energizers often express an openness to others' ideas and projects in a way that is refreshing and appreciated by all the other types. The most outward Energizers are known for being very sociable and good at entertaining. But don't let the entertaining part fool you. They are typically not detail-oriented like most Executives, nor do they throw a perfect party; these Explorers simply create spontaneous, fun moments where people end up being entertained and uplifted. Words or attention grabbers for Energizers are sayings like: "A bunch of us are going over to ..." or "Let's have a party!" Energizers will often be the first to volunteer.

These enthusiastic, people person types live to be happy and feel satisfied. They desire variety but this does not always extend to time being left alone. They typically want to be connected and thrive spending time with others but "struggle through" times when their professional life forces them to concentrate and work in solitude. Often, they will find a friend or family member to tag along with up until they become exhausted, then they need to recharge by themselves so they can be a playful kangaroo once again. As their animal identifier suggests, they like to hop from one fun-packed adventure to another. In fact, they are so drawn to immediate pleasures, they can sometimes neglect their mundane obligations.

Warm, outgoing, and friendly, people are drawn to Energizers because of their simplistic, fun lifestyle. They are literal and realistic and see beauty everywhere, causing them to be happy and desirous of others to share in their delight. They love to live in the moment and do not typically plan things out, nor are they as organized to the degree a Role Model would be. This lack of organization may cause Energizers to overextend themselves to people who request time from them. This can usually be alleviated by the Energizer not only writing down items on their calendar, but then paying attention to it in the future. As Explorers, they like to keep their options open as long as possible, which can frustrate Executives who want the Energizer to nail things down. Energizers also like to constantly generate alternatives to the prescribed plan, in search of a creative alternative that no one else can see. Not particularly hard to get to know nor complicated, Energizers keep things simple, have a zest for life, and love to make people laugh.

Energizers are flexible and believe in taking risks. They recognize value and quality and are prone to leap at good opportunities. Energizers get irritated in a professional setting when they are micro-managed and given too many restrictions. Though the Role Model type thrives when expectations are clearly defined, Energizers do not appreciate as much supervision and prefer to sometimes plunge ahead without knowing all of the limitations to the task. This can bring them unwanted attention or stress at work. Energizers hunger for freedom and action and negotiate easily and quickly. They are sometimes known as free spirits who love to be sociable and entertain others with stories. Energizers, at their best, can be the most generous of the six types, but where they falter is taking on too much which can prevent them from timely follow through. This might lead others to believe they are shallow or scattered.

Another important note about Energizers, since they are

usually happy, open, and not bogged down with burdens, they tend to avoid high maintenance people, especially those who are insensitive and overbearing. Energizers keep their private feelings close to the vest, except with a few trusted advisors and close family members. Though their entire life is like one big drama, they are not drama queens, nor do they like the drama typically associated with overly emotional people. They tend to enjoy keeping things at surface level, which is what helps keep them spontaneous, playful and fun to be around. If not clear enough yet, they do not like to be weighed down with others' heavy emotional problems. To influence Energizers, others need to show them they have listened to them and care for them, being careful not to exclude or gloss over important facts because Energizers have a keen eye for those who might manipulate them. If Energizers perceive you are being sincere, they will readily adapt their behavior or come to an agreement with you.

Some Energizers are not as outgoing and rambunctious as other Energizers. But that does not mean they are not an Energizer; they are still known to "get after" those things they care about, fun included. (Here is an example of why the extrovert/introvert models do not work.) The less outward Energizers may be known as more peaceful, caring, and considerate. These types will possess a little more attention to detail. They are very aware of their environment and may have more niche interests and hobbies they care about. Finally, the more inward Energizers might, at times, seem a little detached from reality, more reserved, and won't open up to others until they are sure they can trust them (which is somewhat true of all Energizers).

Energizers are concrete, utilitarian, enthusiasts. The concrete part means that, like the Role Models, they are more linear in their thinking and perceptions about things, not formulating abstract solutions to complicated problems. They are utilitarian in the basic decisions of life, possessing a positive attitude toward those things that are productive and efficient, and possessing a negative attitude toward those things that are ineffective and useless. Energizers like simplicity and products that work. Who doesn't? But for Energizers it is a real drag when something doesn't work right because it is a complication that takes away their momentary capacity for fun. Though they are in the Explorer family, they are not like Trailblazers, who want to figure out how to fix broken items or spend time wondering about the "why" too much. Life is short, so Energizers have a forward zest that keeps them rolling on with trouble-free items that will not bog them down.

Energizers get stressed when they feel boxed in by obligations or life circumstances, which keep them from spending time with friends. They work best when deadlines are clearly established. This, as with everyone, helps them organize their time. If an Energizer is asked for something, their usual reply is questioning when the item is needed. They are not the most socially cooperative of the six types, which means they will surprise most Executives with their carefree decision-making style. Due to their utilitarian leanings, sometimes they don't mind bending the rules a little bit to make everything work. Yet it is hard to get mad at them when they smile at you with their playful eyes before they are off on their next adventure.

Imminently spontaneous, if an Energizer sees that an investment or product is of good value and can make their life more efficient, then they will jump on the idea, possibly before they have learned all the facts. Energizers hate to be limited by circumstances, especially if it limits their time with those they love. For most people, when they are scheduled to work a shift when their best friends are doing something fun, it is a bummer for them. But for the Energizer, it crushes their soul. They seem to be hardwired to have fun with a good group of friends. They can also be known to work very hard at their vocation or on projects or hobbies to which they are dedicated. In fact, they can be passionate about it to the point that they force themselves to focus on the details and spend time with complex systems. However, this work in the minutia is exhausting for them, and when they complete their tasks, they find they are a little more subdued than normal. Yet, with a little recuperation, or with the promise of a reward or a treat, their exuberance returns, and they can become a buoyant kangaroo once again. In a final analysis, Energizers seem to live by the ancient codes that state whoever brings blessing and joy will be enriched, and one who waters will themselves be watered.

Here is how three different Energizers describe their lives:

Tessa says: *The Energizer profile perfectly describes how I love nothing more than being with people. I am someone who is always down for an after party and ready for the next adventure. While I love going from one plan to the next, I get stressed and rigid when it is anything that I have to plan. I struggle with details, so when I am planning an event, I tend to overanalyze everything and constantly worry about if people are having fun. It takes me away from the flexible, spontaneous person I usually am. I enjoy working on teams; however, I get frustrated when people make things more complicated than they need to be. Simplicity and efficiency are usually my mottos when it comes to tackling a project. The best way to motivate me is by adding some fun into the mix, promising there will be fun afterward, or by allowing me to work in a people-filled environment. Even though I am chatty and can get distracted easily, I am a hard worker who loves to get a job done. I prefer not to be a leader because I find it more exciting to be a follower; nevertheless, I find myself in leadership positions frequently because of my outgoing personality and my ability to relate to many different types of people. My biggest pet peeve is inauthenticity.*

Landon says: *One of the things that I love about being an Energizer is the quest I'm on for happiness. The ability to pursue* *joy is such a gift in my personality, and it helps me feel complete. However, one of the things that I often wrestle with is the weight of what others think of me. If I get the slightest inclination that someone might be upset with me, it can ruin my whole day. At work, the hardest part about being an Energizer is that oftentimes it feels like others aren't pulling their own weight or aren't putting in the energy to do the job well. It bothers me when the team I am part of spends so much time on the details, we don't get to have any fun. As an Energizer, the best way to motivate me is to show me that there is something awesome or fun at the end of the project. I want to be part of something big! Also, truth be told, I'd rather be in charge than follow someone else's vision. Finally, a pet peeve I have is when I feel controlled or manipulated by others. Stop it, I don't like it.*

Clementine says: *I love my personality type because I really resonate with connecting with other people. Asking deep questions and having people share with me all about themselves is one of my favorite things to do. Something that frustrates me at work is when leadership can be kind of hot or cold and unpredictable. It's great to have an amazing leadership team, but when they flip the switch quickly and are all business, and then don't deliver feedback in a good way, it can be frustrating and disappointing. When leaders talk too much about themselves instead of their team, that is also really annoying. Sometimes there is not enough positive coaching and giving of constructive feedback. Leaders need to coach others on a skill set and talk through issues with their employees, not just correct them when something goes bad. Some things that frustrate me in group settings are when big personality types talk too much or talk over people so they can keep talking; or when they don't include others in conversations and have too many inside jokes, this leaves people out. At times, I like to be in charge because it's fun to execute my own specific goals in my job. Other times I like being a worker bee because then the work I do* *can have an immediate result, without waiting on others. It is super important to me to lead by example. One pet peeve I have is when people have a short fuse and have outbursts, trying to take out their frustrations on other people. People who are quick to raise their voice and refuse to listen to other points of view also drive me nuts. When people hold onto grudges and bring it up repeatedly, even when the event happened years ago, that is draining. Let it go. Let's move on and have a healthy relationship.*

It is obvious from these Energizer submissions that the fun factor is huge for this type. For other types reading these paragraphs, take note that to motivate this buoyant type you can promise them something fun either along the way or at the end of the project and they will most likely give you 100 percent effort. Nothing motivates Energizers as much as the promise for fun or a treat.

The four lead traits of Energizers are: (1) Enthusiastic, which means they are vibrant, lively, and pulsing with energy and excitement; (2) Good-natured, which means they are sincere at heart, honest, and vulnerable with trusted friends; (3) In-the-moment, which means they are present, observant, and unencumbered by the past; and (4) Free-spirited, which means they are carefree, uninhibited, and rambunctious.

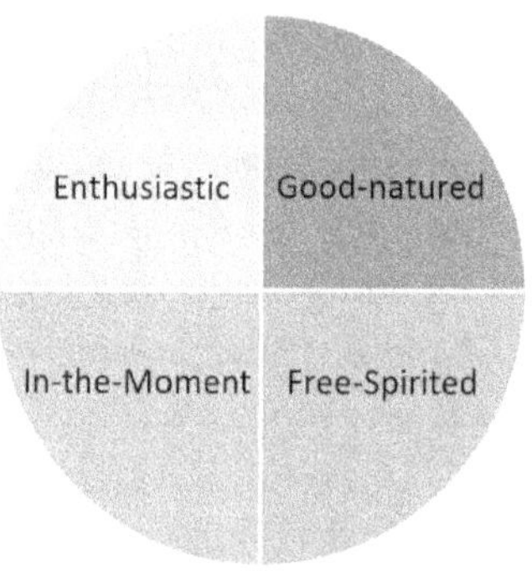

Here is a snapshot of the Energizer type:

Type: *Energizers*

Family: *Explorers*

Hallmark: *Enthusiastic People*

Predominate Goal with Others: *To have fun with others*

Sayings attractive to Energizers: *You only go around once! Variety is the spice of life! A bunch of us are going over to... Don't worry—be happy! Let's have a party!*

Quest 1: *To feel happy*

Quest 2: *Variety*

With a dash of: *Simplicity*

Superpower: *Ability to increase joy in those around them*

Achilles heel: *Scatteredness and superficiality*

Others' perceptions: *Energizers are fun-loving, flexible, and friendly people*

Most: *Spontaneous*

Not too much: *Worried about*

22 Energizer Traits
Energetic
Enthusiastic
Good-natured
In-the-moment
Free-spirited
Vibrant
Enjoys variety
Infectious laughter
Observant
Adaptable
Pulsing w/energy
Spontaneous
Uninhibited
Rambunctious
Positive
Go with the flow
Sincere at heart
Animated
Flexibility
Quest for happiness
Warm
Affirming

details

Worst fears: *Afraid of missing out, being left alone, or forced to do something they don't like*

Energizers want to be seen as: *Fearless and exciting people*

When Energizers are under great stress: *As stress mounts, Energizers are taken over by fatigue and then one failure follows another. Their first reaction to stress is denial. Energizers attempt to stay happy and busy, acting like everything is fine and no one will notice. This overacting makes everyone around them somewhat uncomfortable ... so the Energizer's denial to the issue doesn't work. Like the Role Model, they may try to control anyone or everything around them, but when that fails, fatigue takes over and they are worse off than before.*

How to win their heart: *Take them on a spontaneous adventure, don't make explanations overly complicated, and help them plan the details when they are put in charge of something.*

Famous historical figures who typify the Energizer: *Michelangelo, Peter the Great, Desmond Tutu, Ronald Reagan, Beyoncé, Steven Spielberg, Denzel Washington, Judy Garland, Justin Bieber*

Animal: *Kangaroo*

<u>Strengths:</u>

- Warm, friendly, and upbeat; encourages playful behavior in others
- Eagerness to try new ideas
- Flexibility in group settings
- Can be life of the party and tell interesting stories
- Ability to make routine tasks fun and exciting
- Though utilitarian when alone, on a team they are cooperative and sensitive to other people's needs
- Can find satisfaction in a variety of settings
- Contagious enthusiasm

- Willingness to accept differences and go with
  the flow
- Ability to change gears quickly
- Bold and willing to step out of their comfort zone
- Ability to connect dots well, and bring together
  funny comparisons

<u>Possible Blind Spots:</u>

- Can take on too much, then appear scattered or
  superficial to others
- Will, at times, not follow through on an idea or
  project
- Can feel overbearing or showboating to others,
  especially Executives
- Can sometimes look for more simplistic answers to
  tough problems
- Difficulty working alone for extended periods
  of time
- Tendency to become bored
- Easily distracted
- Tendency to take criticism or negative feedback too
  personally
- Impatience with administrative details
- Tendency to take things at face value and miss
  deeper implications
- Tendency to avoid conflict at all costs
- When overworked, Energizers can become
  grumpy or short, the very antithesis of their usual
  personas

<u>Ways to Grow and Shine as an Energizer:</u>

- Set realistic goals and expectations for yourself
- Consider taking a time-management course

- Follow through on your commitments even if it seems unnecessary at the time
- Find projects you are interested in and volunteer for them
- If you are leading a meeting, set an agenda and stick to it; if not leading, then ask for the agenda ahead of time to be prepared and to help keep you engaged once the meeting starts
- Try not to take constructive feedback personally or get discouraged when things don't go your way
- Pursue making decisions with gusto and sticking with them; this will greatly benefit you in the future
- Seek out support and encouragement from friends when going through a tough time, and don't try to bottle up your emotions
- Use a daily pill box to assist you with needed medications and place it where you can't miss it
- Get help with retirement planning; though it can seem like a long way off, it is necessary to enable your retirement years to be more adventurous

<u>A Few Hints When Dealing with Executives:</u>

When speaking with Executives, try to remember they may not be as jubilant about your ideas as you are. Slow down and try to explain the rationale behind your plans. Assertives may have an especially hard time with Energizers because Assertives are looking to improve the world, but Energizers seem overly content and joyful with how it is right now. Energizers may tire out Executives if they change their mind or the topic of conversation too quickly. Energizers need to slow down when speaking with Loyalists to show them you care about them as individuals and are not just out to get things from them. Energizers irritate Executives when they fail to prioritize work assignments and continually finish projects at the last minute. For a more detailed description of how Energizers interact with other types, see Chapter Nine.

Write down some names of friends who you suspect might be Energizers:

1. ___________________________

2. ___________________________

3. ___________________________

LOYALIST

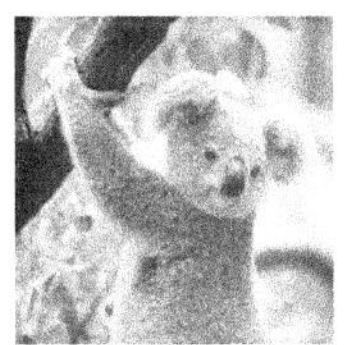

Family   Type

<table>
<tr><td>E
X
E
C
U
T
I
V
E</td><td>R
O
L
E

M
O
D
E
L</td><td>L
O
Y
A
L
I
S
T</td><td>A
S
S
E
R
T
I
V
E</td></tr>
</table>

I would like to introduce you to the Loyalists. Who are these magnificent people and why are they referred to as Loyalists? Well, their name only suggests one aspect of this dynamic type; they are usually intensely loyal, but they also possess many other positive traits. The Loyalists in our society help keep the world running smoothly. They are the peacemakers who are usually agreeable to others and form long-lasting bonds of commitment. Loyalists are tied with Role Models as being the most harmonious of all the personality types. Relationships are extremely important to Loyalists, the building blocks of their lives, and they will fight to keep them.

Loyalists love to be cared for by others and appreciated for who they are. They are extreme helpers who can join a team and fit right in because of their unassuming and self-sacrificing ways. They believe in themselves and the organizations they work for. Loyalists can be smart, witty, and tell amazing stories, but they usually don't mind not being the center of attention and can be happy as a lark not being in management and supervising a lot of people. They are the most patient, welcoming, and accountable people of all six types.

Loyalists are generally very agreeable and conscientious but not the most open of the types. They might take a little longer to get to know as compared to a Role Model, Energizer, or Expressive. Loyalists are competent, consistent, low-maintenance people who are usually tremendously good listeners. They can be comfortable working behind the scenes, and they rarely make waves. When the fighting starts between the other types, these peace-loving people run for the hills, then return when the fighting's over to assist those with the most battle scars. They are devoted friends and family members who also love and support the organizations and causes for which they work. They are hard workers; even after a tiring day at the office they might spend several more hours on a hobby or other commitment.

In case it is not coming through clearly enough, Loyalists are the most unassuming, devoted, and down to earth of all types. They are observant and curious and want to help people in need. In fact, they are so eager to help others and share others' problems that they can take on too much emotionally. The interesting thing about Loyalists is that even though they are good at listening and caring for others, they are intensely private about their own personal lives. It takes more effort to get to know Loyalists than others because they are typically reserved, and not wanting to share their burdens with those around them. This can be a little frustrating for Explorers, especially the Expressives. Loyalists like to keep their lives as pleasant and uncomplicated as possible, and for them this means not opening up to everybody.

Easygoing and relaxed, Loyalists are considered excellent team members who are in touch with their true inner selves. They treasure their free time, and in a fun juxtaposition between the Executive and Explorer family names, Loyalists can be known to love exploring mountain trails, woods, or beaches to discover new things. They love to improve themselves and learn about the world. They are not known to be heavy-handed or take-charge type of people. However, Loyalists readily align themselves with these people and support the "hard chargers" in accomplishing their goals. Working with stronger people reduces their worries about being hurt and increases their sense of self-esteem by feeling protected.

Reassuring and receptive, Loyalists possess a quiet congeniality that endears them to other types. They value rules, appropriate behavior, and look for deeds over words. One area Loyalists should watch out for is an overriding self-effacement that can limit possibilities. What this means is that Loyalists can undersell themselves and downplay their efforts or make themselves feel bad about what they might have said or how they acted. It is important for Loyalists to be positive and possess confidence, even in situations where they might be new or are still learning the ropes. To influence Loyalists, others need to lead by example, and remember that trust and honesty have to be at the core of interacting with them. Their animal is the koala because they exhibit calm, cool waters and are usually not seen as a threat to anyone. Everyone wants to be around these lovable people.

Here is how two Loyalists describe their personality:

Emma says: *I love being a Loyalist. It's in my soul to help people. It makes sense that my job is as a teacher and counselor at a high school. I am energized by listening to others' stories and trying to have encouraging words for them. One thing that might surprise people who know me is that although I find so much value in one-on-one interactions, I could spend days completely alone. I don't always crave relationship time, but I do crave being alone, quiet, and still sometimes. At work, I get most frustrated when my coworkers don't seem to look at the big picture. It's easy to be negative and complain when focused solely on your job, but it seems just as easy to see the positive and be encouraging by looking at what's good for the whole organization. When working in small groups, it bothers me when one person takes up the group's time with irrelevant conversation. I feel like that's not being respectful of everyone's time and not focusing on the group goals. The very best way to motivate me is to show me the end game and explain how I can play a role in that. Tell me how I can help, specifically. I love to do something well that I know is needed and will make an impact. I don't mind being in charge of things when it is something I get to have control over, but I don't want to be the main person running a large organization. I feel like that would take away too much from one-on-one interaction. My pet peeve is when people are negative and not growth minded.*

Bruce says: *As a Loyalist I love fighting for peace and harmony. In a world filled with so much dissension, I want to ease that tension with love. I rejoice when I see people of different backgrounds, ethnicities, and ages come together in friendship. On the other hand, it drives me crazy when someone is unwilling to look beyond their own needs or desires and creates divisions in a group. My greatest motivation comes from being part of a cause greater than myself; something that provides my life with a greater sense of significance. With regard to leadership, I feel a tension here. I would prefer to be in the background but am frustrated when there is a lack of leadership, so I will take up that mantle when there is a vacuum. My pet peeve is when people are flaky.*

THE EXPLORER LOYALIST SUB-TYPE

In the first chapter I explained that one of the personality types had a modification to it that made it somewhat unique, yet not separate enough to be its own personality type. I used the analogy of a planet and a moon instead of two separate planets. So, what is the moon to the Loyalist planet? It is the Explorer Loyalist sub-type. The Loyalist paragraphs above are generally true for both Executive Loyalists and Explorer Loyalists, but Explorer Loyalists operate a little differently than Executive Loyalists in some situations. Executive Loyalists prefer to see issues as black and white and are quicker to make judgements than Explorer Loyalists. Explorer Loyalists, however, like to keep things as uncomplicated as possible, even avoiding people or situations where they suspect they will have to have a serious conversation about responsibilities and obligations. Executive Loyalists are quick to fall in line and obey whatever their supervisor might demand, if within reason. Explorer Loyalists, on the other hand, are constantly on a quest for meaning and purpose and would like to have a greater amount of freedom than simply being told repeatedly what to do. Whereas Executive Loyalists are more orderly and conscientious, Explorer Loyalists gravitate toward flexibility and are not motivated by goals.

Executive Loyalists seek consensus (though they don't like conflict) and will work hard at resolving it quickly so that harmony can resume. In contrast, Explorer Loyalists are not as quick at reconciliation because they are still "processing" the issues and prefer to keep their own council until they figure out a way to move forward or come to peace with the issue. Explorer Loyalists are hard to get to know because they keep their true feelings so deep within themselves. Sometimes even they cannot understand what is bothering them and why they are so reflective about everything. Only a few select friends or a spouse or a sibling can get them to talk about a real concern they might have about their life. However, those who take the time find that Explorer Loyalists possess a type of childlike innocence, and hold a pure, deep love for those they care about.

Complex with their feelings, yet unobtrusive in society, Explorer Loyalists can keep to themselves more than Executive Loyalists, finding beauty and joy in life's simple pleasures. Both types have a dash of introversion, but Explorer Loyalists also have a dollop of inertia. Take it from the author's years of working with both these types, the Executive Loyalist will initially be easier to get to know and work alongside. The Explorer Loyalist might take greater patience and resolve, especially if you come across to them as a hard charger. However, if you can somehow penetrate through their extensive need for privacy and peace, you will find a loyal, lifelong friend who would not hesitate to put their life or reputation on the line for you.

Both types of Loyalists are warm and wonderful people who establish lifetime friendships built on love, respect, appreciation, and of course, loyalty. They seem to abide by an ancient code declaring that a good name is to be chosen rather than great riches; their motto: semper fidelis, "always faithful."

Here is how one Explorer Loyalist describes his personality:

Asher says: *First off, I don't really feel comfortable writing a paragraph like this; I usually don't like being a spokesperson and putting my words out there for the world to see. However, I committed to do this and I wanted to follow through. I think being an Explorer Loyalist gives you a huge step up in life, and if everyone was in the Loyalist family then everyone could just be at harmony with each other and respecting everyone's emotions and boundaries. That seems to come naturally to the people I know who are my type. Specifically, what I like about being an Explorer Loyalist is being more flexible, finding ways to have fun and enjoy life, and finding what really matters. One thing most people probably don't know about me is how much value I put in if people like me or not, even strangers or people that I don't know very well, I find it very important that they have a good perception of me. One thing at work that frustrates me is when other people slacking off creates more work for the rest of the team. I am constantly amazed how little some people care about causing issues in another's life. In group settings and in public something that bothers me is when people talk way too loud on the phone or become attention seekers. I find myself constantly making sure I'm not in others people's way or being a burden and I forget that not everyone is like that. The best way to moti-vate is by telling me that something is important to you or that I would be doing you a favor, I will always go the extra mile to help out those around me. I prefer to follow directions and be a team player when I trust the person leading, but I can be quick to take charge when I feel like I'm the best one for the job. One pet peeve of mine is when other people act too rashly and make impulsive decisions, especially when it comes to relationships. Whenever something happens in my life it usually takes me a while to come to conclusions or decisions because I'm trying to find the best fitting solution. Some advice to get to know me and* *work with me is try to be patient, and give me time. I usually take a while to open up or share my ideas but it helps me when others show they care about my opinion and who I am as a person.*

It is obvious from the contributions that Loyalists love people and are easy to get along with. For other types reading these paragraphs, take note that it is very important to Loyalists, while working in a group, that people carry their own weight and do not cause distractions by being overly negative or critical. Few things motivate Loyalists as much as telling them they can make an impact and truly help an organization or group of people. Also, as the Explorer Loyalist mentioned, authenticity is extremely important to them. If they detect you are prideful or showboating, you will not gain their trust. And last, it is irritating to these more reflective types when one person hogs the conversation in an effort to remain in the center of attention. That is something a Loyalist would never do.

The four lead traits that describe Loyalists are: (1) Welcoming, which means they are friendly, patient, tenderhearted, and considerate; (2) Devoted, which means they are dedicated, helpful, and faithful; (3) Agreeable, which means they are eager to please, unassuming, and fulfilled by assisting others; and (4) Discreet, which means they are cautious and reserved about personal information.

Also, the Explorer Loyalist type is special in that these people not only share the Loyalist traits, but also have four of their own: (1) Comprehending, which means they take time to understand what people are really saying, and give others a chance to be truly seen; (2) Unsystematic, which means they do not operate under a fixed plan and are not overly methodical; (3) Introspective, which means they think deeply on certain issues, are idealistic, and at times can be self-critical; and (4) Unconventional, which means they do not like to conform to the way things are usually done, and they are mostly motivated by their own core values.

Four Lead Traits of the Loyalist

- Welcoming
- Devoted
- Agreeable
- Discreet

Four Lead Traits of the Explorer Loyalist

- Comprehending
- Unsystematic
- Introspective
- Unconventional

Here is a snapshot of the Loyalist type:

Type: *Loyalists*

Family: *Executives and Explorers*

Hallmark: *Welcoming People*

Predominate Goal with Others: *To be at peace with others*

Sayings attractive to Loyalists: *Let's all get along. Go with the flow! May I share something private with you? You have my word on it!*

Quest 1: *To feel authentic and genuine*

Quest 2: *Harmony*

With a dash of: *Introversion*

Superpower: *Ability to be faithful and committed, even in the worst of circumstances*

Achilles heel: *Self-effacement and difficulty disciplining others*

Others' perceptions: *Loyalists are caring, committed, and patient people*

Most: *Supportive (Executive Loyalist), Hate of small talk (Explorer Loyalist)*

Not too much: *Aggressive (Executive Loyalist), Conforming (Explorer Loyalist)*

Worst fears: *Betraying or losing a loved one, not reaching full potential*

Loyalists want to be seen as: *Faithful friends*

When Executive Loyalists are under great stress: *As stress mounts, self-effacement and martyrdom are on the way for the Loyalist. Whatever the issue, an overpersonalization of the perceived crises heaps on tremendous guilt, which could lead to depression. Because Loyalists are the most supportive type, they can easily be taken advantage of. Over time, if not dealt with and stress continues to mount, all of a sudden there can be a volcano of frustration and other emotions that come out, an apparent backlog of what they may have been bottling up for a very long time.*

When Explorer Loyalists are under great stress: *Even at the early stages of stress, Explorer Loyalists, who are usually easygoing, can become non-negotiable and rigid. As stress mounts, they increase in scatteredness, restlessness, and then avoidance. This avoidance will cost them because even mundane but necessary tasks like paying bills, or returning an important phone call can be overlooked, which, in turn, piles up their problems. At its worst, Explorer Loyalists lose their usual quiet demeanor and an "everybody look out or you're asking for trouble!" attitude arises, shocking everyone in the room.*

How to win their heart: *Be kind and considerate, respect their privacy, and apologize quickly and sincerely if you have hurt their feelings.*

Famous historical figures who typify the Loyalist:

<u>22 Loyalist Traits</u>

Loyal
Welcoming
Devoted
Agreeable
Discreet
Patient
Eager to please
Tenderhearted
Nurturing
Unassuming
Cautious
Peacemaker
Understanding
Compassionate
Thoughtful
Faithful
Compliant
Constant
Sympathetic
Congenial
Reassuring
Supportive

Pablo Picasso, Rosa Parks, George H. W. Bush, Mother Theresa, C.S. Lewis, Agatha Christie, Bob Dylan, Queen Elizabeth II
Animal: *Koala*

Strengths:

- Loyal, dependable, and caring
- Can bring calm to a crazy situation
- A strong work ethic
- Extremely dedicated team player who supports the goals of the organization
- Works well with a variety of personality types, even those who are bossy and dominant
- Kind and compassionate to those in need
- Very practical with a strong sense of responsibility
- Thoughtful and attentive to important details
- Warm, friendly, and sensitive people who are supportive and accommodating
- Very devoted to people and organizations in a way that is admirable
- Notices even the smallest details
- Steady and reliable, able to work a task through until accomplished

Possible Blind Spots:

- Can be uncomfortable with power and overly averse to taking risks
- Can be taken advantage of by others
- Tendency to downplay their own efforts and other self-effacing behavior
- Can be inflexible to change unless there is precedence a new way will work
- Sensitivity to criticism; can be stressed out in tension-filled work situations

- Propensity to become discouraged when no longer feeling needed or appreciated
- Tendency to accept things at face value and miss deeper implications
- Strong dislike of overbearing bureaucracy and excessive rules
- Refrain from criticizing or disciplining subordinates, even when drastically needed
- Tendency to internalize negative feelings, bottle up wrongs, walls go up
- Tendency to suffer silently and not reach out for help
- With a reluctance to implement healthy boundaries, can become an enabler of another's harmful behavior

<u>Ways to Grow and Shine as a Loyalist:</u>

- When needing to reprove a co-worker, think of it as a way to greatly assist them by showing them their blind spots
- Seek help to resolve any interpersonal conflicts
- Try not to take things too personally (I know this is easier said than done, but you can will yourself not to be distracted from people's criticisms by focusing on other positive things and diving into your work)
- Find time during the day to recharge yourself, even if you think it is superfluous or lazy
- Assert yourself and let your voice be heard, even in awkward situations
- Try to think about the future, setting goals for five years from now
- Refuse to be manipulated by another person's behavior by implementing healthy relationship boundaries

- Project confidence and be aggressive when looking for a new career
- Remember to ask for meeting agendas in advance; this will accelerate assisting your organization with your ability to study things in depth and look for inaccuracies
- Try to open up more about your feelings with other emotionally healthy people

<u>A Few Hints When Dealing with Explorers:</u>

When speaking with Explorers, slow down and reflect that although they are great at seeing the big picture and potential meaning behind words, they may not actually catch some of the minor details you think are important. When dealing with Trailblazers, they may say something simply to poke or prod without intentionally meaning to harm the Loyalist. Loyalists will probably have the most challenging time with the enthusiastic Energizers, possibly seeing them as flighty and not well-grounded. When communicating with Energizers be direct and straightforward, not getting bogged down explaining complicated theories that will irritate rather than stimulate them. When tempted to become offended by other personalities, remember that all personality types have their strengths and weaknesses. When faced with stressful situations with others, avoid the tendency to become discouraged or distressed. Of all the Explorers, Loyalists may get along best with Expressives. (For a more detailed description of how Loyalists interact with other types, see Chapter Nine.)

Write down some names of friends who you suspect might be Loyalists:

Executive Loyalists

1. _______________________

2. _______________________

3. _______________________

Explorer Loyalists

1. _______________________

2. _______________________

3. _______________________

5

ASSERTIVE

Family			Type
EXECUTIVE	ROLE MODEL	LOYALIST	ASSERTIVE

I would like to introduce you to the Assertives. Who are these incredible people and why are they referred to as Assertives? Well, as their name suggests, Assertives like to assert their will on projects and people with gusto in an honest effort to get things accomplished. These hardworking, responsible people are typically high-achieving goal setters who make things happen. Even if an accomplished task was not on their original to-do list, they might add it later just for the satisfaction of marking it complete. They challenge systems, people, everything in an effort to reform it and make it better.

Though it doesn't apply to all Assertives, they are stereotypically like the first-born child of a large family who doesn't mind taking charge when needed and supervising others. Assertives are often delightful people who love to laugh and tell stories when they are not focused on a task. Although not their animal type in *RELATE*, they are the quintessential busy beavers, taking care of business and accomplishing so much every day that they sometimes do not take time for themselves, which can lead to burn out. Many Assertives have a perfectionistic side to them that drives them on, completing many tasks which is admirable. But sometimes they project this perfectionism onto other people which can lead to relationship stress.

Assertives have high expectations for themselves and others. They are known to speak their minds and tell the truth using candor. Assertives are not known for using extra niceties or flowery language and at times might seem aggressive to others, especially Loyalists. Assertives are so eager to get things accomplished, they may sacrifice being overly diplomatic in exchange for just getting things done. But don't get discouraged with them; at their core they are hard workers simply trying to make a positive dent in the world. Because of their strong work ethic, Assertives make big goals for themselves and push themselves to be better, along with trying to push other people to be their best as well. You might find Assertives running marathons, climbing high mountains, and recruiting others to join them in their achievements.

Assertives are comfortable in challenging others and would not be described as having a lack of self-confidence; in fact, it is just the opposite. They project strength and confidence in a way that bewilders some of the other types. Assertives often find themselves in supervisory positions or are elected team leader by a group. If there is a delay for someone to take charge, the reins may be lost to a self-assured Assertive, but not because the Assertive is power hungry; they just don't want to be adrift and left in a leaderless vacuum. Please hear me out on this, Assertives don't always seek to be in charge; many Assertives are very content letting others lead and wanting to assist them, but deep down they crave excellent leadership, and they don't mind letting people know when they don't see it.

Assertives are hardworking traditionalists who are usually conscientious and rule-abiding. They like to create and enforce order within systems and institutions. They believe that others must earn their trust and prove their worth by being as committed to the organization as the Assertive. Sometimes Assertives might not come across as tactful because the truth seems so obvious and necessary to expose. They do not handle ambiguity well and prefer to bring controversial matters to the surface rather than letting them linger, which in their minds can potentially cause problems down the road. So, to the Assertive, their willfulness and ability to speak directly greatly benefits families and organizations. Their ability to create and enforce order is uncanny, especially with young people.

Assertives see themselves as matter-of-fact people who are easy to get along with. If someone is troubled by something they say, Assertives chalk it up to the other person being a little too sensitive with their feelings. They are sometimes perceived by others as not being overly optimistic because they are willing to speak up and sometimes go against popular opinion; this is merely their perfectionism manifested. Assertives would say they hope to change things for the better and make people and projects the absolute best that they can be, which sounds super optimistic to them.

Eminently fair and judicious, Assertives make decisions based on what makes the most sense at a given time. They are not significantly influenced by how people will feel about, or be affected by, their decisions. Assertives typically have impressive memories for details and can recall with clarity seemingly unimportant events from the past. When they can get into trouble is if they use this knowledge to become argumentative about things because no one has total recall, and they may remember the past differently from others. One interesting item regarding the decision-making of Assertives is that their conclusions seem so obvious to them, and based on fact, that they expect their conclusions to be met with unanimity. They are genuinely taken aback by those who might see things otherwise. Assertives cannot fathom that there could be disagreements or further discussion needed on items that are so clear and defined. Any logical person would agree with this! However, when they verbalize what they think is collective consensus, it is met by a mixture of those who find Assertives overbearing, and others who appreciate people making decisions for the group.

Assertives love people and greatly enjoy being around others, but they are sometimes not very tuned in to the emotional side of people due to the fact that they often lead with their analytical thinking skills instead of feelings and emotions. Because they are highly competitive, and like to be in control of their surroundings, other types might feel as if they have been "handled" a little bit, especially by Loyalists who seek harmony, and Expressives who value connecting above all things. Assertives have limits to their driven nature, however, and they will not sacrifice a good friendship for it. They crave for people to understand that their abruptness is not personal, they are simply trying to accomplish something. They are extremely loyal to people who understand this and still choose to be around them. They think the world would be a much better place if others were like them ... but don't all the types?

Some final thoughts about Assertives—they are not the best at adapting to change. When needing to try new things, with them it is best to use the hit and run approach. Bring up your idea before a decision needs to be made, then reapproach them later to discuss it. This gives Assertives time to absorb the information and adapt it into their own mental process or agenda for the day. They will be much more agreeable to try your idea after they have had time to assimilate it and make it their own. Assertives listen to people who are clear, objective, and confident. They like to find emotional connections through past experiences. For others to persuade them, they need to be credible, direct, and honest. Their animal type is the horse because of the stereotypical image of horses working hard either carrying cowboys, a stagecoach, or machinery on a farm. Horses are known to be dependable, stable, and beautiful work creatures; all of which match the Assertives. They seem to live by the old creed: In all toil there is profit, but mere talk tends only to poverty.

Here is how three Assertives describe their personality:

Isabella says: *I am definitely an Assertive! I strive to be a person who doesn't just represent myself but someone who my family can be proud of and know that I have given my best; a person that my people can call on and know that I'll be there regardless of the situation. Do you need someone to help plan an event? Sure. Do you need to hear the situation from another perspective? No problem. Do you need someone to just be there? Done. What is it that you need? Let's figure out how to achieve it. One thing other people may not know about me is that I strive for perfection, growth, and accomplishment—not just for myself but for others too. This doesn't always play out the way it should, since I can be ignorant* to their feelings. I have to consciously remind myself that my way is not always the best way, and their learning styles, personality types, upbringing, etc., all play a part in the final outcome. I live by the motto: "Do it right the first time." But recognize that there are situations where you need to learn by making mistakes instead of getting it right on the first try. One thing that frustrates me at work is knowing that a coworker or subordinate does not have the drive to excel at everything they do and prefers to do bare minimum to get by. This is frustrating! Everyone has the ability to achieve greatness. It should be something people strive for and only for their personal satisfaction, not for public recognition. In group settings I get annoyed by time wasters. Don't bring up past experiences unless it can be applied to our current situation. If it was similar but can't be used, save the unnecessary details to share after the task has been completed.

The best way to motivate me is to have a plan and be engaging. If you come to me with the end result and have ideas of how to get there, let's do it! I'm all for helping/accomplishing that task. Also, do the research before trying to change things up (i.e., is it even feasible or are we wasting time exploring this new option?). I would much rather be a worker bee instead of being in charge. I am fully content working behind the scenes and not having the spotlight. My dream job is to show up, do what I'm told (to the best of my abilities of course), and go home. No stress! Being in charge is draining. I take issues home and brainstorm how to make it better and it's consuming. I spend countless hours figuring out the best ways to accomplish a task for a certain outcome. No one sees, hears, or is impacted by these struggles except my family. If in charge of a project, perfectionism will keep me up all night, making sure all details are covered. I've tried to do the bare minimum to get a job done and let it be, but my conscience won't allow it.

One pet peeve I have is when there is a lack of order and awareness. I imagine life is like Tetris. You won't always get the right pieces and clear the lines, but if you manage the blocks *correctly and plan ahead, the lines start to vanish. I see it as a task list—sometimes you get everything you need in one shot; task complete. Other times, you have missing pieces, but you're planning ahead, and once that piece comes to you; task complete. If you don't plan, you'll have a mess of unfinished lines and tasks and can feel unfulfilled, like you have wasted precious time. Remember, you don't get to step ten without accomplishing steps one through nine first.*

Edward says: *I feel like my Assertive personality type is very grounded in reality and common sense, which helps me make smart decisions and understand the logic behind most societal norms and rules, and I help contribute positively to the functionality and efficiency of society. Though I may not show it, or use the right words, I care deeply about others and want to help others be happy. I am continuously thinking about others and how my actions will affect others, hopefully in a positive manner. Often, especially when playing games, I will modify the rules to ensure it is fairer and fun for everyone involved, but this can come across (especially to those winning) as unfairly picking sides. I enjoy competition, but not at the expense of someone who is playing and not having any fun. A close competitive game is much more fun than a blowout. One thing that frustrates me at work is when people don't care to do their job to the best of their abilities, no matter how important or insignificant. I will go above and beyond to make sure those things that are my responsibility (and often other people's responsibilities) get done properly, and I take pride in that. So, when people just do the minimum to get by, or just work when the boss is present, or cut corners, it irritates me and baffles me that they have no self-respect or integrity.*

Group projects, at school or work, are the stupidest thing ever because people like me end up doing most of the work, and the lazy bums who do nothing get the same credit just because they're lucky enough to be in my group—because I actually care about the outcome. The best way to motivate me is to give me a project that will actually make an impact or result in improving something, and that's all I need. Busy work or a project that will never be implemented are meaningless. Also, I would rather be in charge because most people (unless they're like me) don't care as much, nor can they figure out how to build a logical pathway, no matter how complex, to complete the objective. Many people just can't see the big picture. And often, the project leader may only be interested in making a show for their boss rather than actually doing a good job just because it's the right thing to do. I used to enjoy watching the TV show The Apprentice with Donald Trump because I couldn't wait for the ineffective bumbling leaders to hear the words, "You're Fired!"

One major pet peeve I have is when other people have no situational awareness of how their actions impact others. Like the driver in the left lane who crosses four lanes of traffic, nearly causing multiple accidents, because they need to make this exit (for which they didn't plan ahead); or people who stop at the top of an escalator because they're looking for directions, without any regard for those behind them; or people who watch a loud movie on an airplane without headphones, oblivious to whether they're bothering anyone else. I could go on and on. These are all rooted in a selfish, self-centered, "I only care about me" attitudes rather than thinking of others and the efficient functioning of society as a whole, even though it may mean an inconvenience for yourself (like going down to the next exit and having to double back).

Christian says: *Assertives say what everyone is thinking but no one else has the guts to say. One reason I love my personality type is that I know that nothing will ever be left unsaid, and the air will always be clear. Something that people may not know is that Assertives do not intend to offend or say things that are meant to be taken personally. At work, there is always a better way to do things, even if it's "the way we used to do it," and timelines are a*

It is obvious from the above write-ups that an Assertive may disagree with others, but it is not to be taken personally. Their incredible need for directness and honesty can come across as too blunt for some, but at their core they truly want to help a project or person. Nothing motivates an Assertive more than to give them a task and then give them time to complete it. Or, better yet give them some co-laborers who can assist them to make the work more enjoyable. Even though many Assertives don't mind working alone and becoming lost in their work to accomplish tasks, they typically also like to be around people, especially those who are contributors. They have great enjoyment when work is being accomplished and there is friendly banter. One thing is absolutely true with this type, it comes down to efficiency. They want things done right, they want things done well, and they hate to waste time.

The four lead traits of Assertives are: (1) Proactive, which means they lean forward into projects, are hardworking, results-oriented and productive; (2) Direct, which means they speak clearly and are straightforward, literal, and skeptical (not easily convinced without evidence); (3) Efficient, which means they have the ability to concentrate efforts on the most pressing needs and reform systems as needed; and (4) Conventional, which means they adhere to accepted standards and like the predictable.

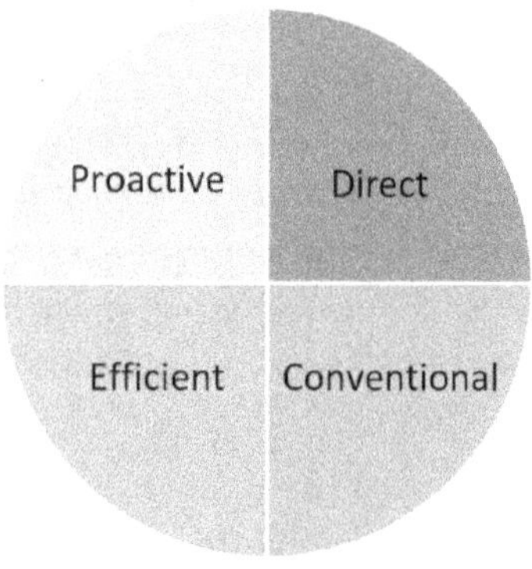

Here is a snapshot of the Assertive type:

Type: *Assertives*

Family: *Executives*

Hallmark: *Proactive People*

Predominate Goal with Others: *Challenge others to do their best*

Sayings attractive to Assertives: *Taking care of business! Work hard, play hard! Anything worth doing is worth doing right! Let's cut to the chase!*

Quest 1: *To achieve*

Quest 2: *To feel supported*

With a dash of: *Perfectionism*

Superpower: *Ability to cut to the chase and work hard day in and day out*

Achilles heel: *Unsympathetic*

Others' perceptions: *Assertives are direct, down-to-earth, strong-willed people*

Most: *Hard-Charging*

Not too much: *Reassuring*

Worst fears: *Afraid of failure and of being seen as lazy or worthless*

Assertives want to be seen as: *Hard workers*

When Assertives are under great stress: *As stress mounts, Assertives become increasingly domineering and refuse to admit failure. Though they try not to display their fear, it becomes obvious to others due to their marked increase in trying to gain control, forcefulness, and inability to acknowledge their own part in creating the stress. They believe a poor decision in times of crises is better than no decision but will blame others for a negative outcome. Because Assertives are usually so in control, their scatteredness becomes unnerving, alarming this usual unflappable type.*

How to win their heart: *Join them in their task and ask them what you can do to help, speak directly and simplify your communication to its basic components. Provide documentation to support your position and give them time to think about new ideas instead of demanding an immediate response.*

Famous historical figures who typify the Assertive: *George Washington, Margaret Thatcher, Condoleezza Rice, Billy Graham, Dwight D. Eisenhower, Warren Buffett, Morgan Freeman, Sean Connery*

Animal: *Horse*

22 Assertive Traits
Proactive
Direct
Efficient
Conventional
Hard-working
Conscientious
Likes authority
Sharp-eyed
Goal-driven
Productive
Logical
Literal
Skeptical
Reformer
Predictable
Determined
Exacting
Firm
Achiever
Overcomer
Hard-charging
Decisive

<u>Strengths:</u>

- Hardworking people who consider details
- Fun to be around when goals are being accomplished
- Valuable work associates who are good at backward planning on big projects
- Self-confident and friendly to others
- Accountable and productive team players
- Willing to step up and take charge when needed
- Ability to focus on one task at a time at great depth
- Possess strong common sense and a realistic perspective
- Ability to recognize what is illogical, inconsistent, or impractical
- Use direct, clear, and easy-to-understand language
- Real-life ability to be honest and trustworthy
- Great at delegating

<u>Possible Blind Spots:</u>

- Can be eager to offer criticisms but slow to speak praise
- Words of truth may hurt others' feelings without realizing it
- The task at hand becomes more important than the people
- Can be impatient, overbearing, insensitive, and too competitive
- Lack of sensitivity to how people will be impacted by decisions
- Unwillingness to change directions and shift gears when needed
- Can "run over" people to get their way

- Difficulty listening to opposing viewpoints without interrupting
- Not overly concerned to invest in relationships unless something is wrong or needs fixing
- Tendency to refuse to acknowledge wrongdoing or to having contributed to a relationship breakdown
- Tendency to be too concerned with social standing or public opinion of them, especially of those they respect
- Inability to deal well with unstructured environments

<u>Ways to Grow and Shine as an Assertive:</u>

- Slow down and consider implications of your decisions on other people
- Though it may be hard to find someone as efficient as the Assertive, look for an effective assistant or secretary who can help keep you organized, remember special events, and find your misplaced stuff
- Be open to new possibilities and try to embrace change
- Change your work setting to create an environment that minimizes interruptions so you can focus
- Seek out and consider advice and opinions from colleagues, especially those with different personality types
- Avoid the tendency to be rigid in your thinking; someone else's new idea might be a great one
- It may not seem a practical exercise at the moment but think about your life as a whole and how you want to be remembered. Look for what is truly important to you and brings value, prioritizing

those relationships and opportunities that bring
you fulfillment
- Work at establishing a rapport with others; instead
of starting a conversation and getting right to the
business at hand, ask others how they are doing
with meaning, and wait patiently for their response
- Try to embrace healthy doses of change, and try to
keep from slipping back into old routines
- Look at the big picture, not just the details; try, at
times, not to have a box. (i.e., Many strive to do
things outside of the box, but try to go even beyond
this.)

<u>A Few Hints When Dealing with Explorers:</u>

Assertives greatest challenges will come from Explorers. Explorers will give profuse constructive feedback if they perceive Assertives are utilizing them as projects. Specifically, Energizers and Expressives can easily become threatened by Assertives' directness and firmness. Their feedback and ideas may not seem realistic nor workable to the Assertive. Assertives need to constantly remember that not everyone brings the same values to work, such as efficiency and practicality; some bring things like humor, creativity, playfulness, and inquisitiveness. Yet, with additional efforts at teamwork, team projects can be much better than if the Assertive had done it by themselves. Assertives will likely have the most perplexing time with Trailblazers. Both types are lead thinkers, and because of this they will challenge each other's creativity and reasons for just about everything. Assertives tend to say what they mean and mean what they say. When others do not take what they say seriously, or if they consistently change, then it creates a significant issue with Assertives. However, what was just described is, to a degree, a "way of life" for Explorers who thrive on changing dynamics. Assertives have a hard time taking others seriously when they are not consistent. They value following through on their word, and they expect the same from others. If other types want to stay on their good side, then they must follow through on their commitments with them. (For a more detailed description of how Assertives interact with other types, see Chapter Nine.)

Write down some names of friends who you suspect might be Assertives:

1. _______________________________

2. _______________________________

3. _______________________________

TRAILBLAZER

Family

Type

EXPLORER

ENERGIZER

TRAILBLAZER

EXPRESSIVE

I would like to introduce you to the Trailblazers. Who are these intriguing people and why are they referred to as Trailblazers? Well, Trailblazers are the quintessential explorers; they want to see what is over the next hill. When walking in a group, you might see them out front, not to be first, but because they yearn to discover what is ahead. Always looking for possibilities, these idealists are constantly generating alternatives for life situations. They love to think of new ideas and new ways of doing things. The Trailblazer brain is always turned on, meaning, it is hard for them to shut it off even when it is time to relax. Trailblazers are the most innovative and independent of the six personality types. They are inquisitive investigators who cannot wait to figure out a solution to a complex problem or come up with a hypothetical scenario to explain what they are talking about. Trailblazers usually make a great first impression and can be very charming. They have a natural gift to get people inspired about their ideas.

One interesting trait of this type is that they tend to love playing practical jokes on others, but not in a mean-spirited way. The goal is to get everyone in on the fun because it displays the wit and creativity of the Trailblazer. Another unique trait Trailblazers have is a major rebellious streak. It annoys the heck out of them to see people blindly following orders without asking questions or debating about it. For Trailblazers, nothing is too sacred to be questioned, scrutinized or laughed about. They will, at times, even debate their own beliefs, or be known to argue with others just for the sake of arguing. Fellow members of the Explorer family don't mind this too much, but sometimes Executives do not consider Trailblazers as well-grounded or practical people. Trailblazers like to come up with ways to do things more efficiently, or to look at life situations a little differently in order to bring humor or needed change to an institution. For the Trailblazer, this is practicality at its finest, offering another way to look at something so that it can become more enjoyable or efficient.

Trailblazers have no issues with considering future implications for things; they love to live in the future and project scenarios to the nth degree if needed to appease their ever-growing thirst for new solutions. Trailblazers can build conceptual frameworks and greatly enhance their organization's current systems. They hunger for competency and knowledge and typically love to be intrigued and challenged by riddles. They are not as fascinated with an abundance of paperwork or meetings that, to them, seem unproductive. Trailblazers compete with Energizers for being the most enthusiastic and spontaneous of the six types. These two types are also similar in that they find life to be one exciting challenge after another.

Trailblazers have a natural knack for leadership. Like Assertives, Trailblazers readily take command of situations when they believe there is a leadership void, yet they don't mind not being in charge ... as long as they have a good leader! This is a consistent theme with all the types; people thirst for worthy leadership. Trailblazers have a low tolerance for incompetence and for those who waste people's time. In leadership, Trailblazers like to establish an affirming, positive atmosphere where value is placed on excellence and results. Trailblazers are visionary leaders who are flexible, dynamic, and see possibilities everywhere. They love to challenge the status quo to find a better way of doing something.

Trailblazers can be charming, charismatic, and even flirtatious at times. Warm and friendly, it is natural for more outgoing Trailblazers to use their bodies to connect with others, often giving a hug, or placing a hand on someone's shoulder. (Note—there is a section on the more introverted Trailblazer type below.) In relationships, Trailblazers possess an idealistic sense which necessitates extra communication from them for two reasons. First, when Trailblazers are relating to a member of the Executive family, they have to especially remember that those personality types are only convinced about an idea if you can show them how something worked in the past. Trailblazers will have to use more than charisma and seek out documentation, perhaps even current research in order to have their ideas seem credible. Second, Trailblazers have to be careful with members of the Explorer family, as well. People are drawn to those with flair and creativity, and it could bring unwarranted friendships their way if they don't tone it down a bit in certain settings.

Trailblazers are skilled at communicating, and, like Expressives, are highly perceptive people who enjoy working in jobs where there is quite a bit of interpersonal interaction. To influence Trailblazers, those who learn to listen to their ideas and acknowledge their expertise or entrepreneurial spirit will be successful. Being overly emotional may drain the Trailblazer type, so provide matter-of-fact examples of how your proposed plan will be successful. Trailblazers will really tune in when you begin with the big picture of why something is important.

Because Trailblazers generally exude high confidence, even in new environments, they may appear condescending or possibly even arrogant to those who don't know them well. Why? Trailblazers are not easy for others to figure out because they do not tend to care too much about outside opinions. Also, they are adaptive and can change their behavior based on what situation in which they may find themselves, so they are a little unpredictable. Most Trailblazers know that their words and actions, at times, might cause some people to shake their heads or judge them, but since they don't care much about what others think, it doesn't modify their behavior. Trailblazers rationalize that they just want to have dynamic conversations and relationships, and if others are offended by that then others most likely have the problem, not the Trailblazer. To truly impact this type, you may need to slow them down, sit with them, and have a knee-to-knee and eye-to-eye discussion, telling them how they personally made you feel.

REGARDING THE MORE INTROVERTED TRAILBLAZER

In an effort to make this assessment as comprehensive as possible, one must consider those Trailblazers who are more reserved and would never be considered a crazy extrovert. A Trailblazer who is a little more inward is even more apt to not be able to turn off their brain. Their minds are always abuzz with ideas and questions, and they will have full-on debates in their head about topics regardless of what setting they are in or who might be around them. In the worst case they might be considered as having paralysis of analysis. In the best case, these intriguing people are mastermind sleuths and love to solve riddles. They can be known to ponder over the mysteries of the universe or theology one minute, then get distracted with simple discrepancies the next. Their mind might fixate on any irregularity with something they are reading, or the conversation at hand.

For those Trailblazers who are more reserved, they might take additional time to speak up, appearing aloof or even akin to an absent-minded professor. Don't be fooled, their mental capacity is such that it can handle multiple strains of thought at the same time. However, it might be hard to put their thoughts into layman's words. To get them to speak, discuss a project in which they are interested, and then you cannot get them to shut up. Because Trailblazers typically do not care about social niceties, they can drift off by themselves or sit alone in public places with relative ease. When given the opportunity, they can spend a good amount of time in a reverie of deep thoughts. Other times they might appear quite engaged and quick-witted.

Those who underestimate the depth and sincerity of a quiet trailblazer will eventually find themselves shocked by it.

One of the things true of the Trailblazer type is that they see and experience the world in a slightly unique way from the other types, typically finding the humorous or ironic side of life and sharing it with others, which can bring joy to those around them. The Trailblazer animal is the fox because, at times, they can be sly, cunning, and mysterious. In their quest for knowledge and feedback, Trailblazers typify the ancient proverb, "…reprove a person of understanding and they will gain knowledge."

Here is how three Trailblazers describe their life:

Gisela says: *It fits that I'm a Trailblazer because I love to ask a lot of questions and find new ways of doing things. The thinking part of me is always turned on, and my brain is constantly generating alternatives. I work well as a team member because I love to come up with new ideas. One thing that frustrates me at work is having to deal with emotions of people who do not get along. It seems simple to me to be nice to others and not say rude things or gossip, but not everyone can follow that. What frustrates me in group settings is when there isn't clear direction from the leader on what to do. I hate wasted time and would prefer to do my own thing than be stuck in an unproductive group. The best way to motivate me is to spark my curiosity, give me minimal guidance, and then let me alone to figure it out for myself. As far as leadership, I like to be in charge, but I think I do my best work when I am number two; it takes the stress off and I can assist my supervisor to help them succeed. My pet peeve is when people are disingenuous.*

Nathan says: *When I read the description for Trailblazers, I felt like I was looking in a mirror. One thing I love about being a*

Trailblazer is my constant desire to explore the world around me and conquer the challenges laid out before me. I feel like it keeps life interesting, and I am always looking forward to my next adventure! One thing other people may not know about me is that, though I come across at times as being indifferent or overly confident towards a personal interaction that may have gone south, deep down I will sometimes dwell on that interaction for days, trying to figure out how I contributed to that negative conversation and what I could have said differently. One thing that frustrates me at work is someone who comes along and tells me something I've started is wrong or won't work. Although, sometimes it strengthens my resolve to prove them wrong! Another thing at work that drives me crazy are users; these are people who won't lift a finger when I'm in need but happily wear me out by asking for, and receiving, favors from me. One thing that frustrates me in group settings is people who aren't real. Actually, that frustrates me in one-on-one interactions as well. In fact, it's one of the few instances when I will cut a conversation short. Also annoying in group settings are people who just like to hear themselves talk and aren't contributing to the group. I think it's safe to say I don't enjoy being around people who waste my time. What motivates me is having a challenge set before me where I'll be able to see the fruit of my labor. I love seeing a job well done. If there is a leadership void, I will step in, and I don't shirk away from management. But I don't necessarily seek out control in interactive situations and am generally comfortable with being a cog in the wheel. But I have an extremely difficult time following incompetent leaders. I would say my pet peeve (besides all those listed above) would be people who don't look me in the eye while conversing.

Colette says: *I love being the Trailblazer because I love analyzing things, running things, and getting everyone on board because I think I have the best way to do it. Most people don't*

It is obvious from the above narratives that Trailblazers don't
mind being in charge if that is the only way to have good leadership. Trailblazers hate wasting time and wither under poor leadership. For other types reading these paragraphs, take note that
even though a Trailblazer may be direct and come off as arrogant or uncaring at times, they do care about others deeply and
will spend days and sometimes weeks thinking about a negative
interaction they may have had and how they might have
contributed toward the problem. Though they are not lead feel-

ers, they can read people fairly well and are aware when they may have offended someone. Trailblazers do not tolerate users well because they are a very productive type, and nothing motivates Trailblazers as much as when they are given respect and appreciation for a job well done. Last, it is clear that Trailblazers can identify disingenuous people quickly and do not tolerate them well.

The four lead traits of Trailblazers are: (1) Adventurous, which means they are spontaneous, adaptable, bold, and creative; (2) Independent, which means they like to be free from outside control, and are self-confident, unpredictable, and entrepreneurial; (3) Inquisitive, which means they are constantly curious and seek to analyze information to form opinions; and (4) Versatile, which means they are resourceful, shows a fondness for changing the status quo, and possesses a bent toward mischievousness.

Here is a snapshot of the Trailblazer type:
Type: *Trailblazers*
Family: *Explorers*
Hallmark: *Inquisitive People*

Predominate Goal with Others: *Inspire and influence others*

Sayings attractive to Trailblazers: *The sky is the limit!*

What if we try this idea? We need a completely original approach!

What have you got to lose?

Quest 1: *Independence*

Quest 2: *To feel respected*

With a dash of: *Self-confidence*

Superpower: *Ability to devise a course of action and lead others to accomplish it*

Achilles heel: *Argumentative and overthink everything*

Others' perceptions: *Trailblazers are intriguing, spontaneous, and creative people*

Most: *Unpredictable*

Not too much: *Rule-follower*

Worst fears: *To lose their independence or for people to hold them back*

Trailblazers want to be seen as: *Competent*

When Trailblazers are under great stress: *As stress mounts, Trailblazers have a bad habit of distorting the facts. Another way to put it is that they begin to speak out of both sides of their mouth and can argue both sides, to a point. Trailblazers tend to attempt to "make up" for stress by talking more and repeating the same sentences, almost as if to try to reassure themselves. As stress increases, Trailblazers become more resistant to ideas from others. Some might call them rebellious; others might call them arrogant. They will seek various ways to avoid stress, but, due to an increase in scatteredness when anxious, they have a harder time than usual orienting themselves out of a tricky situation. When really in a tight spot, Trailblazers may resort to abso-*

22 Trailblazer Traits
Pioneering
Adventurous
Independent
Inquisitive
Versatile
Influencing
Mischievous
Creative
Unpredictable
Action-oriented
Entrepreneurial
Persistent
Problem-solver
Change agent
Pragmatic
Straightforward
Resourceful
Inventive
Impulsive
Self-confident
Challenge status quo
Conceptual

lutes like *"you always"* and can deflect with straw man arguments.

How to win their heart: *Invite them to a mystery event, or, better yet, challenge their creativity by asking them to plan a mystery event, ask them what project they are currently working on, ask for their opinion when faced with a challenge or problem.*

Famous historical figures who typify the Trailblazer: *Abraham Lincoln, Madeleine Albright, Newt Gingrich, Robert Downey Jr., Douglas MacArthur, J. Robert Oppenheimer, Katherine Hepburn, Malcom X, Pink*

Animal: *Fox*

<u>Strengths:</u>

- Intuitive thinkers who generate possibilities and find solutions to thorny problems
- Flexible team players who can work well with a variety of people
- Can work well independently and without supervision
- Creative leaders who can bring together a diverse team and generate a positive atmosphere
- High standards and a strong work ethic
- Excellent communication skills and ability to get others excited about new ideas
- Strong motivation to be competent and excel
- Adaptability; able to shift gears and change directions quickly
- Ability to focus and concentrate deeply on issues
- Enjoyment in initiating and promoting projects
- Can put complex topics into easier to understand concepts for others
- Mannerisms and words can communicate care effectively to others

- Tendency to easily get bored and restless
- Can pick a fight when none exists; can become argumentative when trying to prove a point
- Strong independent streak and dislike of excessive rules
- Impatience with people who they perceive to be unimaginative or incompetent
- Can appear aloof or distracted at times when deep in thought
- Can become defensive when challenged
- Tendency to be impulsive
- Impatience with "social niceties" at some work settings
- Can be blunt and insensitive to the feelings of others
- Tendency to ask too many questions
- Tendency to debate both sides of a topic leaving others bewildered
- Consistency—can tackle many hard projects but suffer sometimes with follow-through

Ways to Grow and Shine as a Trailblazer:

- Work at being patient with people who are not as fast-thinking as yourself, giving them time to comprehend what you are saying and fully express themselves
- Make a to-do list each morning with all of the ideas buzzing around your head, then knock out the most important tasks first
- Follow through on commitments you make with others

- Develop a close-friends mentor group or personal board of directors to critique your ideas and plans
- Tune in to other peoples' needs and work on being compassionate
- Make sure you schedule uninterrupted time to develop your ideas and think things through
- Seek professional development opportunities; take courses or seminars to expand your expertise
- Find time each day to get outside and do something physical
- Recruit and hire an efficient and well organized member of the Executive family to assist you in your career. They might give you a reasonable perspective for your life situations that are not so apparent to you
- Work on being consistent with mind (reading, writing, finances), body (exercise, nutrition, and sleep), and spirit (committing to a spiritual practice and sticking with it)

<u>A Few Hints When Dealing with Executives:</u>

When forced to interact closely with a member of the Executive family, Trailblazers should communicate, up front, how their theory has worked in the past. Show documentation on how your plans have succeeded and Executives will more readily accept your ideas. Some Executives will find your energy level draining. Help them by providing agendas ahead of time so they can see what they are getting into. Loyalists may be exhausted with how Trailblazers attempt to manage so many things at once. Trailblazers will do well to patiently work with others by showing them how your methods could pay off in the long run. On the Explorer side, Expressives may be disillusioned when Trailblazers primarily come off as warm, friendly, and personal, but then fail to take time to develop the relationship further. (For a more detailed description of how Trailblazers interact with other types, see Chapter Nine.)

Write down some names of friends who you suspect might be Trailblazers:

1.______________________________

2.______________________________

3.______________________________

EXPRESSIVE

Family

Type

EXPLORER

ENERGIZER

TRAILBLAZER

EXPRESSIVE

I would like to introduce you to the Expressives. Who are these fascinating people and why are they referred to as Expressives? Expressives love to express their emotions without holding anything back. This can mean usually knowing where you stand with them because their body language and facial expression are good indicators of what they are thinking. These are beautifully creative people who typically excel in relationships and attempt to harmonize people or groups of people.

Expressives are the ultimate people people who love to connect with others. They are optimistic persuaders who love to collaborate and be on a team. They strive for connectedness and work constantly at deepening relationships. For them, relationship work is fun and energizing. Playing a group game or working on a fun project together gives Expressives the time of their lives. They are charmers, idealists, and, at times, ultraspontaneous. They can also be deeply contemplative, especially about relationships or life's other most-important topics.

One of the fascinating aspects about Expressives is how, in a group setting, they seem to be aware of how everyone else is thinking and feeling. Part of this ability is due to their perceptiveness of people and zeroing in on their mannerisms and facial expressions. Another part of this can't be easily explained. Expressives seem to have an acute sensitivity to how people are feeling, and they notice the subtlest of shifts in someone's attitude. They can pick up on expressions and moods quickly and in a way that might be baffling to other types. It is hard to hide your disappointment from them, so be ready to come clean and have an honest conversation about what is bugging you.

Like Trailblazers, Expressives have an insatiable curiosity, which drives them to learn and study, especially if it is in the realm of helping other people. Expressives tend to pride themselves on their uniqueness and individuality. Friendly and usually talkative, Expressives have a wide circle of friends and people they can count on. When alone, or with just one or two good friends, they can be sensitive or sentimental because they are driven by their innermost personal values. However, they only show their inner feelings around people they know they can trust. They are not paranoid, but they are aware that of all the people they attract to themselves, some may or may not have the best intentions for the big-hearted Expressives.

Talkative and articulate, Expressives tend to have the most enhanced communication skills of all six personality types. They are natural counselors who enthusiastically maintain good eye contact and can frequently touch others. Expressives are known to give people an extra squeeze, simply to let them know they are cared for. As you can imagine, this endears a lot of people to them. They make conversation and friendships look easy. They love to talk with people about their personal feelings and discuss their relationships. Though they look right at home in a group setting, often telling stories about past experiences, they also treasure one-on-one times with other people to more deeply grow their relationship.

Expressives are the people in a work setting who somehow grasp what is important to everyone. Their high social awareness stems from an intuitive sense of connectedness with others that grows with each encounter. They are skilled at motivating others with their upbeat attitude and collaborative style. Expressives are committed to unlocking people's potential and see possibilities for others that they sometimes cannot see for themselves. While usually cheerful and connected with others, Expressives can become withdrawn and moody when feeling underappreciated or overwhelmed. To get them back on track, friends can encourage Expressives by showing them the value they bring to organizations and to others.

Expressives are openhearted and open-minded. A good time for them is not just having typical fun at a party. It involves connecting with someone in a special way or bonding with someone over a shared experience. They love heartfelt conversations, and they will come across to others as deep, caring, and creative. In a way, Expressives are the roses of a group setting, possessing an extra beauty and are able to relate to most others in a deeply personal and unique way. People around them will be amazed at how easy it is for Expressives to interact with other people in such a meaningful way, and to metaphorically connect all the dots when in a group. Expressives seem to hold a type of inner composure and joy for relating that is attractive to others. They have an innate capacity to make others feel special, so much that, consequentially, friendships with them deepen fast.

Expressives love it when people present to them a similar passion, authenticity, and desire for connection on projects and plans. At their core, they hold on to an idea of what is right in their mind, and they are willing to sacrifice for it. They possess a certain strength of conviction which is admirable. They feel they must keep a feeling of synthesis where their life has integrity and makes sense to them. To make this even clearer, Expressives want to do the right thing and appreciate it when those around them feel the same way. If they believe in you, and see you treated unjustly, they will stand up for you even at personal cost. Much of the time, to have an Expressive as a friend makes you feel ultraspecial.

Yet Expressives can be super competitive with others as well. It is the intensity and close interaction that gets them going, either on the court or during a board game. If you ever feel a little overwhelmed at their passion during a competition, remember, they are passionate about nearly everything they do; not only in conversations and relationships but playing sports and games as well. If you need evidence of this, watch them cheer for their favorite sports team when a championship is on the line. And they can sometimes get heated with others, but try not to lose heart with them; when the competition is over, they will be back to their good-natured selves, often working doubly hard to restore their friendships and make sure everyone feels supported and encouraged.

To influence an Expressive, others need to challenge their imagination and attempt to show them the big picture when explaining the why to them. Unmask any ulterior motive before speaking with an Expressive, and keep things simple, resisting the use of unnecessary technical jargon and copious details which will turn them off. Remember, Expressives can read other people extremely well, and that is an endearing quality about this type. At their best they use this perceptiveness to aid other people—not destroy them, and it becomes a tool Expressives use to help others see their potential and grow in self-awareness.

Expressives have a collie for an animal type. Dogs are known as human's best friend. Similar to Expressives, collies enthusiastically greet people when reunited (wag their tails, whine, smile etc.). This is the image of the highly relatable Expressive. For them, it is all about relationships and their connections with others. Perceptive and empathetic, social interactions increase their energy level making them even more desirous for others to spend time around. Their contagious friendliness is a gift to the world, and they personally derive great satisfaction from bringing people together and being catalysts for human growth and potential. Expressives typify the ancient proverbs: "… there is a friend who sticks closer than a brother"; and "whoever covers an offense seeks love."

Here is how two different Expressives describes their lives:

Molly says: *My favorite part about realizing that I was an Expressive is that it gave me some words about how I already live my life. Specifically, around being loyal to people and sensing other people's emotions. I love developing deeply personal connections with others, especially people who may be new to our community. One thing that is true about my type, that people don't know,* *is that I despise conflict and will sometimes choke down feelings so that I don't have to talk about the hard stuff. At work, I can be frustrated by unspoken expectations or tension as a result of a work project. It is really important for me that everyone is in good standing with each other. In group settings, my frustration is often a result of a lack of unity; if the group is divided, so am I! The best way to motivate me is to show me how this will help the relationship. I want to be there for the people in my life that matter. While I always have a lot of thoughts about a project, I am probably a better worker bee than being in charge. Mostly because I don't love making tough decisions. And my biggest pet peeve is when someone leaves me out of the conversation. I always want to share my heart!*

Liam says: *I love being an Expressive because it's true how much relationships mean to me. I crave deep authentic relationships with people because I love getting to know the deepest part of who they are. I want to connect with everyone and get to know who their true raw self is, no facades, no disingenuousness. Although I love being around groups of people hanging out, talking, playing games, and "painting the town red," I find greater meaning in spending one-on-one time with someone. I enjoy coming alongside someone who is struggling in life and having real deep conversations and helping them in their journey. Something that frustrates me at work is the reluctancy to change from tradition. I enjoy exploring new possibilities that make things more organized and more enjoyable for everyone. In group settings, I can get frustrated when people aren't socially aware, and they dominate the social flow. The best way to motivate me is to build me up authentically—be real with me, don't be fake. I thrive in an honest environment. While I am fine with being a worker bee, I find myself enjoying being the leader more. I believe my social awareness helps me navigate relationships and figure out which direction we need to go and how to get there. A pet peeve I have is when people will* *not let down their walls, however, I love working with them until their walls fall.*

It is obvious from these write-ups that Expressives love relationships! Finding that deep personal connection with another means the world to them. For other types reading these paragraphs, take note that Expressives crave originality and authenticity. Do not come to them with a hidden agenda, and don't be superficial with them. These are deep people who expect others to reciprocate and share their true selves. This presents a challenge for some people. Expressives also do not want to be stuck in a rut. For them, change is expected and fun.

The four lead traits of Expressives are: (1) Perceptive, which means they are insightful, imaginative, contemplative, and sees possibilities for people everywhere; (2) Connecting, which means they capitalize on all opportunities to deepen relationships; (3) Idealistic, which means they are principled, authentic, value-driven, and thrive on harmony and conflict resolution; and (4) Passionate, which means they easily express affection, and love to persuade, motivate, and impact others.

Four Lead Traits of the Expressive

Here is a snapshot of the Expressive type:

Type: *Expressives*
Family: *Explorers*
Hallmark: *Perceptive People*
Predominate Goal with Others: *Connect others and connect with others*
Sayings attractive to Expressives: *Can I tell you how I feel? There are some people I'd like you to meet! Let's work together and get this done! Anything's possible!*
Quest 1: *To feel significant*
Quest 2: *To deepen relationships*
With a dash of: *People pleasing*
Superpower: *Ability to perceive how others are thinking and feeling*
Achilles heel: *Overcommitment and struggle to make tough decisions*
Others' perceptions: *Expressives are warm and charming and deeply care about people*
Most: *Optimistic*
Not too much: *Follow through*
Worst fears: *Losing a significant relationship and not finding answers to life's big questions*
Expressives want to be seen as: *Loving*
When Expressives are under great stress: *Normally easygoing, with an increase in stress Expressives become moody and irritable. This tendency can lead to extreme sullenness and a "woe is me" attitude. There can also be blind denial to a bad situation. When given enough data that things are not great, a highly emotional response, even leading to bitterness or an "I'll get even" feeling, sometimes erupts. Most of the guilt they generate is heaped on themselves, and this can lead to a stressed Expressive*

22 Expressive Traits
Communicative
Perceptive
Connecting
Idealistic
Passionate
Discerning
Inspiring
Optimistic
Interpersonal
Insightful
Imaginative
Contemplative
Originality
Dramatic
Sensitive
Impactful
Pleasing
Charming
Interactive
Persuasive
Generous
Motivating

having physical maladies that accompany the stress because these sensitive types feel things so strongly.

How to win their heart: *Sit down with them and have a heart-to-heart conversation about an important topic, be honest with them if you are ever disappointed, help them out by organizing something in their life like paying bills or tidying up the garage.*

Famous historical figures who typify the Expressive: *Mark Twain, Aldous Huxley, Martin Luther King Jr., Walt Disney, Orson Wells, Jennifer Aniston, Tony Blair, Oprah Winfrey, Bono*

Animal: *Collie*

<u>Strengths:</u>

- Enthusiastic, warm friends who love people and cherish relationships
- Ability to connect with almost anyone, even the unlovable
- Optimistic persuaders with strong people skills
- Creative collaborators who work well on teams and bring cohesion
- Remarkable ability to brighten another person's day
- Genuine interest in others and ability to help others grow and develop
- Eagerness to take risks and try new things
- Uncanny perceptiveness about people's moods, needs, and desires
- Charismatic leadership and ability to build consensus
- Deep commitment to work they believe in
- Generous, not only with finances but truly magnanimous in heart wishing others to succeed
- Feel honored when others open up to them

<u>Possible Blind Spots:</u>

- Can sweep problems under the rug and bury issues in denial to ignore unpleasantness
- Though good when working through conflict resolution, may avoid potential conflict too long
- Can carry grudges and induce guilt in others
- Perfectionistic attitude can hinder teamwork
- Difficulty setting priorities and making decisions
- Reluctance to do things in traditional ways
- Tendency to be disorganized
- Tendency to idealize people and relationships
- Impatient working with institutions or with people who are too rigid
- Trouble disciplining subordinates with objectivity
- Become discouraged when people don't measure up to high expectations
- Intense desire to please others which can compromise judgment

<u>Ways to Grow and Shine as an Expressive:</u>

- Work at following through on commitments and being positive around people, even if you dislike or disagree with them
- Though you dislike the tried and true way of doing things, consider traditional methods as a way to approach a new task before jumping in
- Find one or two friends who will speak candidly with you; let them know how you are feeling on a regular basis, asking them for brutal honesty
- Try not to be so hard on yourself; focusing all your mental energy on how you might have screwed up is unproductive and can spiral you downward

- Make a list of life priorities and set realistic goals to accomplish them
- Take things less personally and try not to get involved in personality conflicts between co-workers when it doesn't involve you
- Consider becoming a trainer or coach
- Try not to listen to just one point of view
- Volunteer in an organization that will energize you
- When you begin your day, take five to ten minutes to think through how you will accomplish all of your most important tasks, especially the ones you've been putting off that have deadlines attached to them; and when life feels out of control ask a friend to assist you with this discipline

<u>A Few Hints When Dealing with Executives:</u>

Expressives tend to match well with Role Models and Loyalists, but an Expressive child, spouse, or subordinate can suffer emotionally when paired with an Assertive parent, spouse, or boss. These two personality types are nearly exact opposites. In this situation there needs to be plenty of opportunity to hear each other out and seek understanding. The Expressive needs to speak clearly about what they think and try to give precise, logical reasons why they are doing things. Though challenging, the Assertive needs to try to listen with patience and understanding and provide reasons for why they are asking seemingly demanding things from the Expressive (like for their child to keep their room neat and tidy). If Assertives slow down and give more verbal assurances in everyday tasks and praise the Expressive, the Expressive will respond better when critiques on bigger issues need to be given. As for Explorers, an Expressive will also find it challenging to relate with Trailblazers who tend to speak what is right on their mind, potentially casting a cloud on the incredibly optimistic and people-oriented Expressive. Like Assertives, if Trailblazers slow down and give more verbal assurances and praise to the Expressive, the Expressive will respond much more positively. (For a more detailed description of how Expressives interact with other types, see Chapter Nine.)

Write down some names of friends who you suspect might be Expressives:

1.____________________________

2.____________________________

3.____________________________

Key Talking Points
EXPRESSIVE

Abstract Thinker * Perceptive and Passionate * Enjoys Going Deep with Others

A SUMMARY OF THE SIX PERSONALITY TYPES

This graphic illustrates the approximate percentages of the six personality types. (Chapter Eleven reviews the contents in the bubbles: Meticulous, Harmonizing, Utilitarian, and the Z factor.)

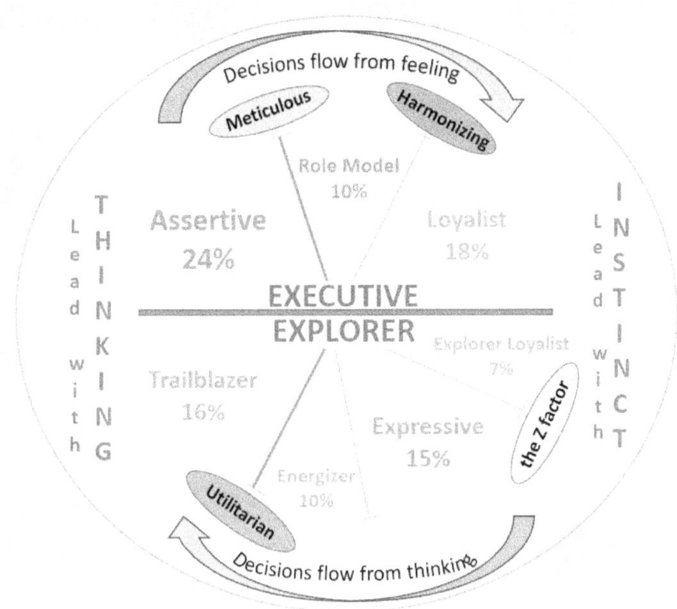

This table summarizes some of the key characteristics of each type:

Personality Type	Animal	Hallmark	Predominate Goal w/Others	Quest 1 & Quest 2	Achilles Heel	Want to be Viewed as:
Role Model	Eagle	Responsible People	Eager to help others	Belonging Feel valued	Guilt creator	Confident
Energizer	Kangaroo	Enthusiastic People	Have fun with others	Feel happy Variety	Superficiality	Fearless
Loyalist	Koala	Welcoming People	Be at peace with others	Feel authentic Harmony	Self-Effacement	Faithful
Assertive	Horse	Proactive People	Challenge others	To achieve Feel supported	Unsympathetic	Hard-working
Trailblazer	Fox	Inquisitive People	Inspire others	Independence Feel respected	Argumentative	Competent
Expressive	Collie	Perceptive People	Connect others	Feel significant Feel connected	Over-commitment	Loving

This is a cumulative personality inventory with 22 traits for each type (as presented in respective chapter):

ROLE MODEL	ENERGIZER	LOYALIST	ASSERTIVE	TRAILBLAZER	EXPRESSIVE
Exemplar	Energetic	Loyal	Proactive	Pioneering	Communicative
Responsible	Enthusiastic	Welcoming	Direct	Adventurous	Perceptive
Trusting	Good-natured	Devoted	Efficient	Independent	Connecting
Considerate	In-the-moment	Agreeable	Conventional	Inquisitive	Idealistic
Cooperative	Free-spirited	Discreet	Hard-working	Versatile	Passionate
Dutiful	Vibrant	Patient	Conscientious	Influencing	Discerning
Appropriate	Enjoys variety	Eager to please	Likes authority	Mischievous	Inspiring
Enjoys challenges	Infectious laughter	Tenderhearted	Sharp-eyed	Creative	Optimistic
Polite	Observant	Nurturing	Goal-driven	Unpredictable	Interpersonal
Competitive	Adaptable	Unassuming	Productive	Action-oriented	Insightful
Purposeful	Pulsing w/energy	Cautious	Logical	Entrepreneurial	Imaginative
Settled	Spontaneous	Peacemaker	Literal	Persistent	Contemplative
Accountable	Uninhibited	Understanding	Skeptical	Problem-solver	Originality
Tolerant	Rambunctious	Compassionate	Reformer	Change agent	Dramatic
Diplomatic	Positive	Thoughtful	Predictable	Pragmatic	Sensitive
Attentive	Go with the flow	Faithful	Determined	Straightforward	Impactful
Steadiness	Sincere at heart	Compliant	Exacting	Resourceful	Pleasing
Persevering	Animated	Constant	Firm	Inventive	Charming
Diligent	Flexibility	Sympathetic	Achiever	Impulsive	Interactive
Dependable	Quest for happiness	Congenial	Overcomer	Self-confident	Persuasive
Consistent	Warm	Reassuring	Hard-charging	Challenge status quo	Generous
Harmonizing	Affirming	Supportive	Decisive	Conceptual	Motivating

Now that we have looked at all six personality profiles, here are a few snapshots to learn more about the differences of each type. These *light-hearted* comparisons are below. Please do not take them too seriously.

1. The type of transportation each type relates to
2. A response to four questions
3. A profession that begins with the letter "S"
4. Time stamps for each type

Personality	Vehicle	Reason
Role Model	*A pickup truck*	*A useful vehicle which can help others*
Energizer	*A hot-air balloon*	*Adventurous way to experience the world with new perspective*
Loyalist	*A gondola ski lift*	*A safely connected, peaceful ride, protected from the weather*
Assertive	*A bulldozer*	*A way to dramatically improve the world around them*
Trailblazer	*A rocket ship*	*A way to explore worlds beyond this one*
Expressive	*A sports convertible*	*An intimate, enjoyable ride for two*

RESPONSE TO FOUR QUESTIONS

If one were to ask each personality type a familiar question—"*If a tree fell in the woods and no one was there to hear it, would it make a noise?*" Here is a sample answer for each personality type:

Personality	Response
Role Model	*Of course it makes a sound, is this a trick question?*
Energizer	*Wait a minute, what did you say happened in the woods?*
Loyalist	*Well, I feel like it would make a noise, but whatever you decide is fine with me.*
Assertive	*I don't have time with these pointless discussions!*
Trailblazer	*Why is it that you get to ask the questions?*
Expressive	*Are we best friends?*

If one were to ask each personality type this question—"*Why didn't you say 'I love you' to me this morning?*" Here is a sample answer for each personality type:

Personality	Response
Role Model	*Oh, my bad, I will get you next time.*
Energizer	*Wow, does someone need a hug? Come here!*
Loyalist	*Oh, I'm so sorry, I must have been distracted.*
Assertive	*You are too sensitive.*
Trailblazer	*Is that a new requirement? I don't mind saying it, I just want to know your expectations.*
Expressive	*I had no idea how important that was to you. I definitely love you, and I will make sure I say it every day from now on!*

If one were to ask each personality type this question—"*What makes the world go around?*"
Here is a sample answer for each personality type:

<u>Personality</u> <u>Response</u>
Role Model *Love*

Energizer *Happiness*

Loyalist *Keeping your promises*

Assertive *Getting things accomplished*

Trailblazer *Technically the answer is the earth is spinning on its axis, but other than that, probably money*

Expressive *People realizing their potential, or two people fully connecting*

If one were to ask each personality type this question—"*If you could ask your future self one question, what would it be?*" Here is a sample answer for each personality type:

<u>Personality</u> <u>Response</u>
Role Model *What job am I doing?*

Energizer *Where am I living?*

Loyalist *Who am I married to?*

Assertive *What have I achieved?*

Trailblazer *Do we have affordable flying cars yet?*

Expressive *Have I found my soul mate?*

OCCUPATIONS THAT BEGIN WITH THE LETTER "S" (this is much more light-hearted than serious)

<u>Personality</u> <u>Vocations</u>
Role Model *Statesman, Scheduler, School teacher, Surgeon*

Energizer *Sports announcer, Skateboarder, Stunt double, Scuba diver*

Loyalist *Social worker, Switchboard operator, Shopkeeper, Soldier*

Assertive *Sniper/Sharpshooter, Sheriff, Surveyor, Supervisor*

Trailblazer *Scientist, Scout, Sleuth, Seismologist*

Expressive *Salesman, Socialite, Screenwriter, Sculptor*

Role Model	*Present---Call me any time and I will help you out.*
Energizer	*Present---Let's make the most of the time we have now.*
Loyalist	*Past---This is the way we've always done it, why change it?*
Assertive	*Past---Show me proof that your way has worked in the past!*
Trailblazer	*Future---Let's see what happens when we try this.*
Expressive	*Future---Just cherish me from now to eternity.*

FIVE HELPFUL HABITS AND ONE KEY MOTIVATOR FOR EACH TYPE

Role Model

1. Check your calendar before responding "yes" to someone; this will assist you with priorities and to not overcommit.
2. Put your phone away at least thirty minutes before you go to bed to help unwind; talk to someone else, read, or meditate/pray.
3. Consider, for a moment, what is really important in your life and decide to make a change which might impact the world.
4. Reflect on a situation in the past twenty-four hours where you may not have shown leadership and could have responded better to a situation. A.k.a. a plan to exert greater courage when a similar situation arises.
5. If you don't already have one, find a mentor or life coach. Though it may not be possible to discuss things together each day, you could benefit from writing notes to yourself about which to speak to this person when you do meet. Be intentional about sharing your current triumphs or struggles and seek out their counsel.

One key Motivator for the Role Model

One key motivator for Role Models is the desire to help other people which, in turn, makes the Role Model feel valued. They want to serve others and do good things for family and close friends. Role Models like to be liked and work to make it happen. To motivate them, ask them if they can assist with an important project that would truly help others.

Energizer

1. Send a quick note to a favorite friend and tell them you miss them or say thank you.
2. At some point, when free, play one of your favorite songs and dance around.
3. Think of one of your long-term life goals, try to break it down into smaller objectives for each week, and decide what it will take each day to stay on target this week.
4. Think of a situation at work where there may be conflict—to identify whether you are dealing with the situation head-on or avoiding it. Take action steps to push through potentially painful encounters.
5. If you don't already have one, find a mentor or life coach. Though it may not be to discuss things together each day, you could benefit from writing notes to yourself about which to speak to this person when you do meet. Be intentional about sharing your current triumphs or struggles and seek out their counsel.

One Key Motivator for the Energizer

One key motivator for Energizers is to experience something new and exciting. They want to be wowed and thrilled in new ways and be provided new challenges in which to conquer. To motivate them, introduce an Energizer to a new adventure. This might seem simplistic, but it works for them.

Loyalist

1. Each night before bed, put away the phone and write in a journal about the events of the day.
2. Spend some time outside, enjoying the weather and scenery, even if it's more comfy inside.
3. Prioritize the three most important things to get done before the end of the week.
4. Think of a situation at work where there may be conflict to identify, whether you are dealing with the situation head-on or avoiding it. Take action steps to push through potentially painful encounters.
5. If you don't already have one, find a mentor or life coach. Though it may not be possible to discuss things together each day, you could benefit from writing notes to yourself about which to speak to this person when you do meet. Be intentional about sharing your current triumphs or struggles and seek out their counsel.

One Key Motivator for the Executive Loyalist

One key motivator for Loyalists is the desire to live by their values which includes being loyal to family and close friends. They prioritize based on what they think is right and important, and will stick by others, even to their detriment, if they are inspired to do so. To motivate a Loyalist to do something, explain to them how the activity will increase harmony and loyalty within the group you are working in.

One Key Motivator for the Explorer Loyalist

One key motivator for Explorer Loyalists is to become more authentic. They don't want to participate in anything just to go through the motions. The only things worth their time are activities where people can be genuine and where they don't feel rushed.

To motivate them, give them plenty of time and space to reflect and contemplate.

Assertive

1. Even when in a rush, before asking someone for something, genuinely ask how they are doing first to express care, and truly digest their answer.
2. Before bed, make a list of the most-important tasks for the next day to ease any anxiety and to help you rest better.
3. Take a moment to evaluate your current, most-important relationships and consider how you might encourage these people by writing them a letter (or notecard) or do something else to make them feel appreciated. It is good to communicate care regularly.
4. Slow down. Take a moment for yourself to meditate or pray. Perhaps take a walk outside. This habit should be done especially when you are most busy.
5. If you don't already have one, find a mentor or life coach. Though it may not be possible to discuss things together each day, you could benefit from

writing notes to yourself about which to speak to this person when you do meet. Be intentional about sharing your current triumphs or struggles and seek out their counsel.

One Key Motivator for the Assertive

One key motivator for Assertives is the desire to be dutiful and to reform situations to make them more efficient. They want to do good deeds and be seen as good people, and they will challenge systems and other people to make it happen. To motivate them, tell them you will support them in achieving an important task for the organization in which you are working.

Trailblazer

1. Once each day take five to ten minutes and sit in silence to allow your mind to decompress. Take this moment to tune into what you are currently thinking and feeling. What is racing around your mind? What is your body experiencing? The thought here is to settle yourself.
2. Tackle "the" project you do not want to do and have been putting off; getting it out of the way greatly relieves stress and increases joy.
3. Read at least a chapter a day in a book that interests you. Make notes to yourself on things that you want to remember.
4. Consider who you might have argued with that day and how any impatience on your part might have played a role. Evaluate how you can better manage that relationship in the future.

5. If you don't already have one, find a mentor or life coach. Though it may not be possible to discuss things together each day, you could benefit from writing notes to yourself about which to speak to this person when you do meet. Be intentional about sharing your current triumphs or struggles and seek out their counsel.

One Key Motivator for the Trailblazer

One key motivator for Trailblazers is the desire to advance and explore, and not just new trails in the physical world; they crave mental exploration as well. They will ask questions ad nauseum if their curiosity is piqued. Typically, they love history and figuring out how things work—now and in the past. To motivate them, challenge their mind, especially in the area of how to advance a concept or develop a new model.

Expressive

1. Write down all the thoughts racing around in your mind at the end of the day in order to help you relax and sleep better.
2. Remind yourself of all the great aspects of where you are and what you're doing now to increase joy.
3. Think of one of your long-term life goals, try to break it down into smaller objectives for each week and decide what it will take each day to stay on target this week.
4. Consider with whom you might be annoyed that day and how any impatience on your part might have played a role. Evaluate how you can better manage that relationship in the future.

5. If you don't already have one, find a mentor or life coach. Though it may not be possible to discuss things together each day, you could benefit from writing notes to yourself about which to speak to this person when you do meet. Be intentional about sharing your current triumphs or struggles and seek out their counsel.

One Key Motivator for the Expressive

One key motivator for Expressives is the desire to do something significant such as assist others in the area of relationships. They want to make a positive dent in the world and help humanity in the realm of relationships and connecting people more deeply. To motivate Expressives, ask them for help with a current relationship issue within a family or set of coworkers.

⑨

HOW EACH RELATE TYPE INTERACTS WITH EVERY OTHER TYPE

Role Models and Energizers

Though not in the same family of personality profiles, Energizers are one of the types more complementary in nature to the Role Model type. Both communication styles like to deal with the concrete, meaning what is practical and real. The Role Model will appear slightly more grounded and serious than the Energizer. The Energizer will come across slightly more adventurous and fun-loving than the Role Model. Energizers love to live for the moment, not always taking into consideration the consequences of making a spontaneous decision without all the facts. This will take additional patience for the steadier Role Model. How can Role Models help the adventurous Energizers with decision making? Role Models believe that duties and responsibilities should come before personal fun and relaxation. By appealing to the Energizer's sense of fun and adventure, a Role Model can help the Energizer see that if they work hard before they play hard, then they can play even harder and enjoy life more stress free. At first, the Energizer may find that the Role Model's need for calm and control stifles this ever-buoyant kangaroo type. Energizers do not like rules or routines, and this can interfere with the Role Model's quest to be dutiful and socially cooperative, but the Role Model tends to give the Energizer good grounding.

A helpful part of this pairing is how both types hate conflict and desire harmony. The Energizer type likes to diffuse tension in difficult situations as soon as possible because, for them, a big, ugly confrontation is unappealing and takes away from their joyful and carefree style. It is better to use humor and charm and quickly avoid negative emotions. This trait is a gift to the Role Model who also craves to keep things sorted out so harmony can reign. The bottom line here is that the Role Model gives the Energizer an excellent grounding by keeping their expectations in the real world, while at the same time the Energizer livens up the Role Model and keeps them playful. Energizers learn to appreciate the stability and protectiveness of the Role Model type, and Role Models learn to appreciate the fun nature and adventurous antics of the Energizer. Overall, this pairing does not have the significant hurdles of some of the other types. In this you've been given a gift. Enjoy each other.

Role Models and Loyalists

Of all the six types, the Role Models and the Loyalists are the most closely aligned. One of the few differences between them is that Loyalists are typically more reserved, and Role Models are a little more action oriented. Role Models can be extremely talkative and voice their feelings easily with others. They have strong views of right and wrong and don't mind expressing them to others. The Loyalist's world might be described as being more self-contained than the Role Model's world. This won't cause too much strain because Role Models are one of the most sensitive types regarding irritating others. With their twin goals of helping people and harmonizing with others, Role

Models will quickly pick up on clues if they are being too chatty or too active for the Loyalist. Also, Loyalists are the best at listening and being patient with others; therefore, Loyalists are not typically an annoyance to Role Models or, for that matter, any of the types. Role Models might become impatient with the methodical and/or reflective style of the Loyalist, so Role Models will need to work at being more patient and respectful. Though both types like to be careful, correct, and thorough, Role Models come across a little more perfectionistic; Loyalists come across more peaceable.

Though both types are driven for completeness and perfection, many Loyalists can be happy with a 90 percent solution. But this is not so with every Role Model; they have an intense drive to understand something and get it right. This need for a 100 percent solution can be aggravating to those around them and will definitely increase the patience level of the Loyalist. One caution, since most Loyalists are more private with their feelings, a Role Model might offend them and not realize it. Role Models might incorrectly assume that the Loyalist will bring up something hurting them. But Loyalists are the most reflective of the six types and might be processing the necessity to make an issue out of something bothering them. It will take an observant Role Model to learn to pick up on this and engage the Loyalist when they feel something is hurting them. Overall, Loyalists and Role Models usually become best friends because they have similar value systems and are loyal, caring, and other-centered.

Role Models and Assertives

These two types generally get along well. Role Models and Assertives are both in the Executive family so there are many similarities, along with a few differences between them. Role

Models have good interpersonal skills and do not offend others easily. But not all the types move within relationships as fluidly as Role Models. There are times when an Assertive might hurt a Role Model's feelings by saying what they think. The good news in this pairing is that Assertives and Role Models are both concrete thinkers and socially cooperative. This means that they like to discuss what is tangible and solid and speak literally. They also are generally agreeable in their relations with other people and like to adhere to societies' prescribed methods of functioning. For instance, both types contain a zest to improve the world and become an important, hardworking part of the process.

Where the two types will run into an issue is how Assertives tend to lead with their thinking skills, and Role Models tend to lead with their feelings. Assertives need to remember that Role Models take practically everything personally and can be easily offended. This sensitivity doesn't mean that Role Models are too emotional; it means that they take relationships so seriously that when there is a perceived slight it can really infiltrate the Role Model's thoughts and make them sullen. In an Assertive/Role Model marriage it is important to remember that since words can easily hurt, there needs to be clarity. The following advice might sound ultraobvious, but it works: If the Role Model ever feels offended or disrespected, they need to ask the Assertive what they meant by a specific statement. Assertives are usually eager to clarify things they have said and take ownership of it. In the ebb and flow of these exchanges, Assertives will learn to respect a Role Model's feelings and will learn to avoid accusing them of being irrational. In a similar vein, a Role Model must learn to respect the Assertive's need for directness and not constantly accuse them of being mean or rude. Not every setting will lend itself to wasting time with flowery language, and in many cases speaking directly is a gift. These two types usually get along famously when they work through this key area.

Role Models and Trailblazers

In this interesting pairing there is a chance to become a dynamic duo, but the first potential friction point is that the Trailblazer may become despondent due to the Role Model's lack of interest in trying new ideas. There is also an issue with hurt feelings and emotions. Trailblazers need to understand that Role Models can take nearly everything personally. Trailblazers also need to understand that it's not only with content, but the way things are said, that can hurt feelings. It doesn't mean that Role Models are too emotional; it means that they take relationships so seriously that when there is a perceived slight it can infiltrate the Role Model's thoughts, and they can become sullen. In a Trailblazer/Role Model marriage it is important to remember that since words can easily hurt, there needs to be clarity. The following advice might sound painstaking, but it works; if Role Models ever feel offended or disrespected, they need to ask the Trailblazer what they meant by a specific statement.

Trailblazers can learn to respect a Role Model's feelings and avoid ever accusing them of being irrational. In a similar vein, Role Models can learn to respect the Trailblazer's need for directness and not constantly accuse them of being rude. Another item, though Trailblazers are gifted with coming up with new pathways, they need to be careful that if their proposal does not align with the Role Model's value system, the Trailblazer will need to spend extra time explaining the importance of their desired end state. Role Models typically love to talk and discuss things. They may find that the Trailblazer needs a break after listening to a story or two. Conversely, there are times when the Trailblazer has a lot to say, and they love to hear feedback on their ideas. This is a great time for the Role Model to not only engage the Trailblazer on their ideas but bring in some of the Role Model's ideas as well. When discussing a sensitive issue, it will help Trailblazers if they bring up a point of agreement to the Role Model before bringing up a point of contention. This will build a bridge toward greater understanding and mutual respect. Overall, these types get along well once they appreciate the differences and work hard to minimize friction points.

Role Models and Expressives

In watching these two types operate together, there is a mutual appreciation and trust from the beginning because both truly care about others and are willing to work hard to have positive relationships. Role Models assist others by offering practical suggestions, and real-world help like dropping off groceries. Expressives tend to help others by deeply associating with their needs, and feeling another's burdens as if they were their own.

Members of the Expressive type flourish in trying new and unusual ideas, which is not a hallmark of Role Models who prefer the tried and true. In time, this can really frustrate the Expressive. Conversely, Role Models love to stick to deadlines and be organized in how they approach matters, which is not a pattern of the Expressive. In time, this can really frustrate the Role Model. Both types need to work hard to explain why the way they do things is not wrong, or ill-advised, and explain it in a constructive manner. Expressives might use the phrase, "Variety is the spice of life." Role Models might tell the Expressive, "It is the early, and organized, bird who gets the worm." Both are true. Role Models may also struggle to get Expressives to make choices and decide on a course of action. Role Models simply need to remind Expressives that the decision can be changed later with new data, and it is not set in stone forever. This helps the idealistic Expressive move forward.

Expressives, as part of the Explorer family, can be highly creative and enthusiastic. Role Models need to be careful not to put a damper on Expressives by consistently pointing out flaws in their logic. Expressives can help Role Models find creative pathways in life where none seemed to exist before (at least in the eye of the very practical Role Model). In order to persuade an Expressive, Role Models need to provide relevant facts which speak toward the big picture and idealistic nature of the Expressive. It is best to engage an Expressive's values and spark their imagination. In order to persuade a Role Model, Expressives must be personal with them, and present ideas with uncomplicated rationale. Keeping things practical and positive, it is best for the Expressive to lead by example; show their Role Model friend how something is done (in their methodology), and if it makes sense to the Role Model, they will readily work it into their routine.

Role Models and other Role Models

It is a unique pairing in a relationship set to have two people assessed into the same personality profile, in this case Role Model and Role Model. One has to probe a little deeper about communication between the exact same types. First off, you are likely to feel a strong connection with each other based upon your fundamental similarities: pragmatism, correctness, and an eagerness to please. You both tend to feel most alive when you get out and experience the world around you. Both of you are warm, friendly, and people-oriented, so there is appreciation and understanding in this relationship pairing of Role Model and Role Model. Where disagreements will play out will be on the finer points because you both love to share details about your lives and talk about connecting points in your history.

You are both energetic communicators and will eagerly attempt to tell each other about things going on in your lives. It is important to remember that listening is a gift to be given daily, not just on someone's birthday or at Christmas. When one is sharing, do not simply plan out the next thing to say, but give the gift of true listening. Both of you are warm and people-oriented with a high value system; you can rely on the fact that you can trust each other and have each other's backs. But what will you argue about? The little things like the temperature in the room, and which music, movies, and television shows are the best. Usually both will like to be well organized and tidy in your living space, but sometimes things get left undone and become messy, and that can make a Role Model a little frustrated. You probably fall into a routine about which chores are done by whom, but when one is stressed or overtired, a Role Model can neglect certain things on their to do list. The items that can cause friction in any pairing are driving habits, mannerisms, messiness, and how one may go about day-to-day chores. When one Role Model does criticize the other Role Model, it is taken as an affront—a very serious offense. Along with the Loyalist Loyalist relationship, these two types have a tendency to bottle things up and bury issues, preferring to overlook stress and continue to live in harmony. Advice for this pairing is simple: don't bottle things up, don't keep a record of mistakes, share them willingly with your partner before you go to bed each night. This personality type is very receptive to another person coming to them in honesty and authenticity. Communicate often and keep the fires burning. With regular gardening of the relationship, your partner will be your home base, supporting you for a lifetime.

Energizers and Loyalists

In one way, these two types are far apart, particularly with the level of exuberance Energizers display. Energizers constantly attempt to pull people into fun projects, but Loyalists might offer Energizers quite a challenge. Energizers are out in the world, actively seeking friends with whom to do things. As utilitarian experiencers, Energizers usually test the limits, seeking to be efficient, and to find new pathways. Loyalists, on the other hand, are socially cooperative and conscientious, not wanting to rock the boat but to do things the way they are supposed to be done—the way others have done them in the past. Energizers are not worried about the past as much as the present and how much fun they might have today. As you can see, this creates a dilemma between the types. However, with a little patience and understanding, these types can assist each other.

What they have in common is their desire for close relationships and harmony. Loyalists take their responsibilities very seriously. They can help Energizers to slow down and consider the implications of their decisions, and Energizers can assist Loyalists with having variety, being creative, and being in motion. The Loyalist might be tempted to lose heart at times because Energizers can drain them. But, if both types keep pathways of communication open, use candor and are respectful, this personality grouping can have a lot of fun together with deep appreciation of their differences. Loyalists have a tendency to underestimate their own value. Energizers, with their upbeat attitudes, can encourage the Loyalist to think more highly of themselves. Loyalists can assist Energizers with setting long-term goals, seeing the importance of meeting deadlines, and being a compliant rule-follower once in a while.

In communication, it is important for the Energizer to respect the amount of time and thought a Loyalist needs before having an important conversation. Loyalists might even need some alone time to gear up for a negotiation or family meeting. Energizers are so spontaneous, they might enter into a very sensitive subject area without thinking much about it, nor be prepare to talk specifics. A cautious and private Loyalist should resist immediately thinking the Energizer is insincere, even if they did not begin the conversation with details or in a way that is more subdued and respectful. For both types, actions speak louder than words, and enjoying activities together (like gardening, cooking, or sports) is a great way to increase intimacy and build each other's self-esteem.

Energizers and Assertives

Initially, these two types can drive each other somewhat batty. Assertives, with their truth-speaking, can be a little blunt for the feelings-based Energizers. Energizers, with their quest to test the limits and have a risky adventure, might seem a little rash to the logical and steady Assertive. Energizers will learn to appreciate that Assertives do love people and want to have close relationships, and Assertives will learn to appreciate that an Energizer's spontaneous idea can be fun and bring good memories. Assertives might find Energizers too chatty and tiring to be around for extensive periods of time. Energizers will most likely find Assertives too reluctant to try new ideas and break the rules a little bit. Assertives might consider Energizers too inconsistent and sensitive. Energizers can assist Assertives with softening their bluntness and instruct them in how to better care for the more emotional personality types. Assertives like to spend time reflecting before acting, in complete opposition to the Energizer type. Assertives can help Energizers slow down and consider the implications of their actions. Energizers can help Assertives by teaching them that sometimes the moment to strike is immediately, before all the data is in. Assertives, who by nature are one of the most responsible types, can assist Energizers with being more serious and accountable about their future commitments. Assertives listen to people who are clear, objective, and confident. They like to find emotional connections through past experiences.

For Energizers to persuade Assertives they need to be

credible, direct, and honest. To influence Energizers, Assertives need to lead by example and show Energizers that they have listened and care about them. A final note on this pairing, Energizers crave harmony and do not like conflict. Assertives crave for people to walk the walk and follow through with what they say they will do. When an Assertive does not see consistency in an Energizer, they will be tempted to call them out on it. The Energizer has a choice to make; if they choose not to be offended and realize that this is the Assertive's way for greater closeness, honesty, and consistency, then this relationship pairing will bloom. Likewise, when Energizers do not feel appreciation or harmony from an Assertive, they will be tempted to call them out on it. The Assertive then has a choice to make; if they choose not to be offended and realize that this is the Energizer's attempt for greater closeness, then this relationship pairing will doubly bloom.

Energizers and Trailblazers

This grouping has potential to be a super match; yet at times they can get a little feisty with each other. With both types being members of the Explorer family, they have a lot in common. What needs to be worked out is that Energizers are more sensitive and feelings-oriented. Like the Assertives, Trailblazers have a tendency to be blunt and speak before they consider the ramifications of how their words will impact people who desire a high level of harmony. More than any other type, Trailblazers generate alternatives and new ways of doing something. However, Energizers are not as impressed with new and unusual ideas like Trailblazers and Expressives; they are more into thrills and having fun. Yet Energizers and Trailblazers can relate in both being utilitarian decision makers and delight in finding the most efficient way to do tasks. They like to keep things simple.

These two types are not as concerned about rules and being socially cooperative as the other four types. Thus, together they are dangerous to have in charge because they can rationalize just about anything if they think their method is an improvement. They might project a veneer of respecting authority, but then (wink wink) they are off, hiking on an unauthorized trail or stretching the limits of the law somehow. To influence Trailblazers, Energizers need to listen to their ideas and acknowledge their expertise and entrepreneurial spirit. Being overly emotional may drain the Trailblazer type, so Energizers do well to provide matter-of-fact examples of how their plan might be successful. Trailblazers will really tune in when you begin with the big picture of why something's important. To influence Energizers, Trailblazers need to be careful not to exclude or gloss over important facts and should resist from using big words that sound overly important. Energizers want people to be real with them, but mostly they want to have fun. These two types can have a lot of fun together—with tons of laughter and frivolity—but it might be wise to have an Executive friend along who can incorporate some guardrails on their adventures.

Energizers and Expressives

Energizers and Expressives are the second closest pairing of the six types behind the Role Models and Loyalists combination. They share all the key ingredients of the Explorer family, such as being incredibly optimistic, how they handle difficulty, and seeing power through a relational lens. Most significantly, both types are super skilled at forming and keeping relationships, so deep bonds typically develop between these personalities. What makes these personalities distinct mostly comes down to two areas: how they communicate, and how they cooperate in society. In communication, Energizers are concrete communicators. They like to talk about what is going on at the moment and what is immediately at hand. They can make decisions easily with little planning. Expressives are generally more idealistic and abstract communicators; this means Expressives will talk about what something or someone is becoming, and they can see life as an intense drama. Both of these areas can, at times, go right over the Energizer's head, since they are chiefly concerned with the present and what's real and practical. Expressives speak about values and ideals; they are creative, looking for silver linings, and one-of-a-kind relationships. Being utilitarian, Energizers don't use flowery language nor spend much time looking for the deeper meaning behind things.

In society, Energizers have an easier time being rule breakers if a rule doesn't make sense to them. They are utilitarian decision makers who try to do things the best way to achieve their goals, with less regard for social concerns. Expressives try to do the right thing and are more concerned with the social aspects of their activities. Though the types are similar, there are plenty of opportunities to learn from each other. Energizers might learn to appreciate some of the deeper aspects of life and be more thoughtful in considering life choices. Expressives might learn to become more playful, less contemplative and moody about things, and take events for how they appear on the surface. Not everyone is out to help you or destroy you (the idealist mind); there are a lot of people simply interested in having fun like the Energizer kangaroo, putting very little thought into how their words or actions might affect others. In time, with mutual appreciation and respect, these two types can synergize and become a powerful force in their community.

Energizers and other Energizers

It is a unique pairing in a relationship set to have two people assessed into the same personality profile, in this case Energizer and Energizer. One has to probe a little deeper about communication between the exact same types. First off, you are likely to feel a strong connection with each other based upon your fundamental similarities: being straightforward with each other, wanting to experience an adventure, and a desire to enjoy the moment and have fun. You both tend to feel most alive when you get out and experience the world around you. Both of you are genuine and thoughtful people so there is a wonderful camaraderie in this relationship pairing of Energizer and Energizer. Where disagreements will arise will be on the specifics of things because you both love to share details about your lives and talk about the many adventures you have had. You are both energetic communicators and will eagerly attempt to tell each other about issues going on in your lives. It is important to remember that listening is a gift to be given daily, not just on someone's birthday or at Christmas. When one is sharing, do not simply plan out the next thing to say but give the gift of true listening.

Both of you are cheerful and people-oriented, truly loving the spontaneous events in life, and enjoying the moment. Since you are both so versatile and carefree, you will have fun discussing the more rigid people in your lives and share curiosities about what makes others tick. So, what will your pairing argue about? The little things like driving habits, the temperature in the room, and which music, movies, and television shows are the best. Neither one of you place much value on being organized and tidy over having fun and interacting with people; you will get to your chores later. Energizers can rest in that decision because they usually do get their chores done, and quicker than other types. The other items that can cause friction in any pairing are the details in life like who will pay the bills, mannerisms, messiness, and how one may go about day-to-day chores. When one Energizer does criticize the other Energizer, these carefree types usually find a way to laugh about it down the road, after the stress of the moment is gone. Speaking of stress, when Energizers are under heavy stress, they attempt to stay busy and produce the same output as usual, which typically fails.

Like several of the other types, Energizers have a tendency to bottle things up and bury them, preferring to overlook stress and continue to live in harmony. Advice for this pairing is simple: don't bottle things up, don't keep a record of mistakes, share them willingly with your partner before you go to bed each night. This personality type is very receptive to another person coming to them in honesty and authenticity. Communicate often and keep the fires burning. With regular gardening of the relationship, your partner will be your home base, supporting you for a lifetime.

Loyalists and Assertives

Loyalists and Assertives are not too far apart. Both belong to the Executive family, so they are similar in how they deal with certain areas of life, such as how they use power, deal with difficulty, and process data. What separates them is how they go about implementing their views. For Loyalists, the most peacemaking personality type, they will continue to build bridges even when it is obvious the other person no longer cares for them or wants to abide by their rules. Assertives don't have that need. Assertives are so black and white with how others should act; if the other person is not being agreeable or sticking to prescribed boundaries, then the Assertive has no problem issuing an ultimatum and following through with it, no matter what results may come. Loyalists are more concerned about the impact of the relationship and possess a heavy desire to keep peace as long as possible.

In a Loyalist and Assertive relationship, the Loyalist will usually go with whatever the more assertive Assertive wants. Assertives are achievers who need to feel as if they are making a difference each day and accomplishing something. Loyalists like to make a difference as well but are not as driven as Assertives; thus, they will go with the flow more often. Loyalists feel protected around strong personality types, so they often end up around an Assertive type. Where they need to be careful is not to allow their own identity to become swallowed up in another person (of any type). Loyalists are unique, wonderful people who have their own voice. They should be allowed to express themselves freely and be heard. However, their meek and gentle style keeps them from wanting to push this area and make needed changes. These two types usually function well in relationships because both like to keep boundaries clearly defined and both love to make goals and constantly move forward to achieve them. In an Assertive/Loyalist parenting relationship, the Assertive parent may wonder why their Loyalist child is more reflective or hesitant about making decisions and taking action. In fact, Assertives may become impatient with the slower moving Loyalist. The Loyalist is not out to take on the world and accomplish everything possible in one day. They tend to move at their own pace, and sometimes pick and choose at length how they want to accomplish a task. With patience, however, these two types can learn to tolerate and appreciate their differences.

Loyalists and Trailblazers

Trailblazers will, at times, mystify the thoughtful Loyalist. The seemingly irreverent things that the Trailblazer says or does might be frowned upon by the more conservative Loyalist. Trailblazers are not as concerned with other people's opinions or feelings as a congenial Loyalist. The number of questions the Trailblazer will generate toward a Loyalist will be draining for them. Before these two types hang out together, a wise Loyalist will anticipate the flood of questions and activity and gear themselves up to spend time being interviewed as soon as the Trailblazer arrives. Trailblazers will be wise to rein it in a little bit, and not do all the talking. Loyalists tend to be gentle, soft-spoken, and unassuming. No one would describe a Trailblazer this way. The more outgoing Trailblazer type (some Trailblazers are more reserved) have been known to dominate an entire group discussion by asking probing questions to get people talking. When others dominate a conversation, it really grinds a Loyalist's gears. Trailblazers will do well to remember that Loyalists first and foremost value their own and other peoples' feelings. Trailblazers should not consider this a weakness but a strength.

Also, Loyalists like to think through things before taking action. This can be annoying for the decisive Trailblazer type. Loyalists can assist Trailblazers in slowing down to consider facts and small details before moving into a decision prematurely that might have second- or third-order effects. Normally, Trailblazers see the big picture, understand the options available to them, and want to move ahead quickly. Therefore, Trailblazers can assist Loyalists by showing them the benefit of moving forward on projects when time is of the essence, instead of waiting for a perfect scenario. Trailblazers can also model how being driven or ambitious is not a negative trait when done with intentionality and concern for others. The key for the Loyalist is to feel valued. When in a relationship, if the Trailblazer slows down to consider the concerns of the Loyalist, it will pay off in big future dividends.

Loyalists and Expressives

Expressives and Loyalists share the fact that they base much of their lives on how they feel about things. Also, they both value doing things the right way and they usually cooperate with social norms. Where they differ is that Loyalists tend to internalize their feelings, whereas Expressives typically externalize them. Expressives use their intuition and are usually driven by their conceptions or even fantasies. This mode of operation might be a little scary for Loyalists who tend to stick with the tried and true—things that have been proven over and over. Expressives are spontaneous, optimistic, persuaders who see potential in everyone, including the Loyalists. Loyalists are—no surprise—the most loyal of the six types, unassuming, and can sometimes be artistic. Expressives can assist their relationship with Loyalists by remembering not to overwhelm them with big ideas and try to provide more relevant facts.

To influence Loyalists, Expressives need to lead by example, and remember that trust and honesty need to be the core of interacting with them. Loyalists can assist in their relationship with Expressives by not hiding the way they feel, and not feeling guilty when they attempt to persuade an Expressive to do something for them. To influence an Expressive, Loyalists need to challenge their imagination and attempt to show them the big picture when explaining the why to them. Unmask any ulterior motive before speaking with an Expressive, and keep things simple, speaking without technical jargon and too many details, which will turn them off. Lastly, it is important to remember that Expressives are quick, impulsive, and enthusiastic about most things; Loyalists are a quieter type, have an incredible store of knowledge, and shun the limelight. When these two types work together on a project, they can do really well by tapping into each other's strengths, resources, and synergizing their various styles instead of seeing them as a wedge.

It is important in this pairing for the Expressive not to get dismayed when sharing their dreams and visions with the Loyalist. Loyalists like to see ideas work in practice, and not spend too much theorizing about the unknown, or interpreting the meaning of things. Because Expressives tend to be more verbal in their communication than Loyalists it will be important for Expressives to slow down and attempt to draw out what Loyalists might be thinking. Loyalists usually don't mind that Expressives do more of the talking, but they do want/need to be heard from time to time to feel valued and an important part of the relationship.

Loyalists and other Loyalists

It is a unique pairing in a relationship set to have two people assessed into the same personality profile, in this case Loyalist and Loyalist. Though the Loyalist type and the Explorer Loyalist type have some easily observable differences, one has to think a little deeper about communication between the exact same types. First off, you are likely to feel a strong connection with each other based upon your fundamental similarities: a strong sense of right and wrong, an eagerness to please, and a perpetual desire to serve and assist others. Both of you are warm, friendly, and people-oriented, so there is a mutual love and respect sort of "baked-in" with this relationship pairing of Loyalist and Loyalist. Where disagreements will play out will be on the technicalities of things because you share a general interest in pragmatism, correctness, and discreetness. In fact, because this type is a little bit more reserved than the other types, there will be a closeness shared between the Loyalist and Loyalist, knowing they can trust each other, they have each other's backs, and that there is 100 percent confidentiality between them.

But what will you argue about? The little things. Toilet paper rolls, driving habits, mannerisms, and how one may go about day-to-day chores. Also, one might easily become the enabler of the other one with their bad habits or addictions, very hesitant to criticize their mate or make the issue public. When one Loyalist does criticize the other Loyalist, it is taken as an affront—a very serious offense. These types have a tendency to bottle things up. When in a stressful situation, perhaps regarding finances, living situation, sex, or in-laws, the stress can build up and all of a sudden there can be a volcano of frustration and other emotions that pours out, an apparent long-standing buildup of what may have been bottled up for a very long time. The ability to deeply wound each other in this relationship is possible because it will be seen as a betrayal of your shared understanding of the world, other people, and how you have lived in the past. Advice for this pairing is simple: don't bottle things up, don't keep a record of mistakes, share them willingly with your partner before you go to bed each night. This personality type is very receptive to another person coming to them in honesty and authenticity. Communicate often and keep the fires burning. With regular gardening of the relationship, your partner will be your home base, supporting you for a lifetime.

Assertives and Trailblazers

This is quite the matchup! Assertives and Trailblazers will appreciate each other and confound each other. As lead thinkers, these two types can speak directly to each other without too much fear of hurting each other's feelings. Candor for both types is key, and they can usually get to the heart of an issue fairly fast. However, it is important for each to remember that the essence of true candor is to say things with love at an appropriate time. Speaking hard truths at inappropriate times can be downright rude and obnoxious. There shouldn't be any "front-stabbing" with candor; it is to be chiefly used for another's good. Where Assertives and Trailblazers differ is in how they see the world and what is important to them, which is just about the whole of our existence. Trailblazers are abstract, utilitarian, influencers who are not too concerned about doing something simply to be socially expedient. They truly don't care what people think. For this pioneering type, pragmatism is the key; doing what is most efficient, even if it upsets the applecart. Trailblazers use their intuition and thinking skills to find better ways of performing routine tasks. If no way exists, they invent a pathway, then readily recruit others to join them.

Assertives, however, are socially cooperative and concrete thinkers, which means they generally accept societies' prescribed methods of functioning and don't use their thinking to bend the rules or get away with things. What triggers the self-confident, hardworking Assertive is when they see inconsistencies in someone's logic, or sense that someone is all talk and no walk. To gain the Assertive's respect, the Trailblazer has to be the real deal. This is a Trailblazer challenge because their freewheeling style may not seem genuine at times. Trailblazers, with their optimistic enthusiasm, might come across to Assertives as not being sincere. Trailblazers have to work hard at showing Assertives that their methods are workable and often can bring a lot of fun. Assertives have to work at giving Trailblazers the benefit of the doubt and not be skeptical when an idea seems out of sync with their values. Just because an Assertive cannot conceptualize what the Trailblazer is describing does not mean it should not happen. However, not all Trailblazer ideas are good ones, and when an Assertive challenges them, Trailblazers need to keep from getting bent out of shape. Hear out the Assertive, they similarly have good ideas. Trailblazers can learn a lot from Assertives if they slow down and consider the sensibility of the Assertive's idea. Many times, the best course of action isn't what is most fun and exciting, and Assertives are great at pointing out what is realistic and practical. Assertives and Trailblazers both yearn for credibility and consistency, and working together they can make these important values a reality. If it is not clear enough yet, Trailblazers will need to slow down and explain thoroughly to Assertives how some of their ideas are practical and can work and not become discouraged with resistance. Assertives, likewise, have great ideas that are usually tried and true; however, they will need to fight against how their personality puts up immediate resistance to new and untested ideas when coupled with a Trailblazer. This matchup can work. It takes a lot of effort. When successful, the results are phenomenal and this team in unity can take on the world.

Assertives and Expressives

Assertives and Expressives seem miles apart, but that doesn't mean they cannot have a meaningful relationship bringing joy and contentment. Assertives typically keep things on a more cerebral level and sometimes can appear unaware of emotions and feelings of others. This can present quite an issue with the emotionally expressive Expressives. The Expressive will do well in this matchup not to take personally any criticisms or rejections of their ideas. They need to remember that Assertives are not out to get them, nor destroy them. They are just more candid and truthful than most types. Expressives would do well, when working with Assertives, to prepare themselves for resistance to their ideas, or a critique of their reasoning and logic. Reminding themselves of these issues ahead of time will help the Expressive not to get defensive or feel threatened by an Assertive's direct questioning or severe tone. Expressives will need to go out of their way to show Assertives that their proposals are realistic, workable, and specific because Assertives are generally thorough, painstaking, and systematic.

While interacting with an Expressive, Assertives will sometimes need to be intentional to patiently listen to an opposing viewpoint, which might be difficult at the moment. Assertives need to work at remaining open to input from the Expressive, not jump to conclusions, and also be responsive when an Expressive shares their heart with them. This will take effort, but the rewards are great. When Expressives feel listened to they feel appreciated, and an appreciated Expressive is ultrarewarding. Listening to Expressives and repeating back what they are communicating means the world to this highly relational type. To become close to an Expressive, Assertives have to open up. This is hard for most Assertives. They do not mind sharing about past experiences or present problems, but to share about how deeply they feel about a specific subject may seem silly to them. There are times when Assertives will open up, and certain things really strike them profoundly. It is at these times that they would be more prone to share about their emotions. This takes patience and determination on the part of the Expressive. However, the longer you relate to an Assertive you find that there are deeper layers, and there really are emotions down there, profound and genuine. It takes a patient Expressive to get to that point, but it is worth it. One last note, the above paragraph sounds like there are insurmountable obstacles accosting this combination of types, but it is not true. As mentioned at the beginning, many Assertive/Expressive pairs have found great joy and contentment together, and they would have it no other way.

Assertives and other Assertives

It is a unique pairing in a relationship set to have two people assessed into the same personality profile, in this case Assertive and Assertive. One has to probe a little deeper about communication between the exact same types. First off, you are likely to feel a strong connection with each other based upon your fundamental similarities: pragmatism, process, and correctness. Both of you are hardworking, results-oriented, and productive, so there is a mutual love and respect sort of "baked-in" with this relationship pairing of Assertive and Assertive. You will believe that each other is a strong, upstanding citizen who cares about getting things done the right way, no matter how long it takes. There will be a certain shared joy that each is accomplishing something significant when working on a project together because both are excited about improving their piece of the world. This includes improving the little nit-noid things around them that are not functioning well.

Since you are both honest and straightforward, you are eager to honor your commitments. If married, separating will not be in each other's vocabulary because of the nature of this values-driven type. One thing that will be important for this relationship to succeed is to remember to compliment each other. Duty-oriented Assertives are the least type that needs a compliment, but that is precisely why you should give compliments freely. You are each usually working hard behind the scenes, often doing things most people don't care to do. Recognize that gift in each other and call it out. Though a compliment isn't necessary, it is sure nice to hear once in a while to feel appreciated for all the hard work that is done. Also, listen fully and completely to each other. It is important to remember that listening is a gift to be given daily, not just on someone's birthday or at Christmas. When one is sharing, do not simply plan out the next thing to say but give the gift of true listening.

Both of you are levelheaded and do not get especially hurt

when one of your beliefs is challenged. However, since both of you are likely to operate more from your head than your heart, it is important to take time to develop the emotional side of life together. Talk about your inner feelings once in a while and hurts you may have or have had. Try to go deeper in demonstrating compassion and empathy for each other. Life is more than the perfunctory tasks of getting things done each day. Assertives don't need romance, but why not experience it? Take delight in buying flowers or gifts for each other and creating intimate interactions. It can be fun to partake in areas outside of your normal functioning. Where disagreements will come will most likely be on the specifics of your memories on past experiences; who said what, when, and for how long something happened. Seems ridiculous, right? But it happens a lot. So, what will your pairing, and nearly every other pairing, argue about? The little things like driving habits, the temperature in the room, and which music, movies, and television shows are the best. The other items that can cause friction in any pairing are the details in life like who will pay the bills, mannerisms, messiness, and how one may go about day-to-day chores. When one Assertive does criticize the other Assertive, it often comes across as super direct and forceful. There can be bumps in the road and some stress until you learn about which things are most important to each other, which items you will leave alone, and which items are hills to die on. Speaking of stress, when Assertives are under heavy stress they become increasingly domineering and refuse to admit failure. A fellow Assertive can use directness and call them out on it. Communicate often and keep the fires burning. With regular gardening of the relationship, your partner will be your home base, supporting you for a lifetime.

Trailblazers and Expressives

Trailblazers and Expressives can have a lot of fun together. They can also get on each other's nerves at times. These two types have many similarities. Because Trailblazers and Expressives are Explorers, their world is out there, and they readily seek to embrace new concepts and ideas. They both can visualize potentialities that do not yet exist, and then run eagerly toward them with gusto. Where the two types differ is in how they utilize feelings in relationships. Trailblazers can come across, at first, very genuine and sincere in relating to an Expressive. But as time moves on and the Trailblazer is not as sensitive, Expressives feel like the Trailblazer may not be as deep as they once thought. What is happening is that Trailblazers tend to make their decisions based on what is logical, regardless of how they or others may feel at the moment. This doesn't mean they are shallow; it means Trailblazers, who enjoy having many close friends, sometimes overextend themselves in directions where their dynamic style draws people closer than what they might consider appropriate after some consideration. Expressives do this as well, but they are simply more diplomatic at breaking things off and having healthy boundaries. Trailblazers are direct and will use bluntness, when necessary, not especially caring if someone might get their feelings hurt by their comments.

Another difference is that the Trailblazer is utilitarian, and the Expressive is socially cooperative. This means that an Expressive is more apt to please others and follow generally agreed upon societal rules. Trailblazers seem to follow a code of their own, which may or may not align with what the norm may be in a particular situation. Frankly put, Trailblazers simply don't care about trying to please others. They generally believe they know what's best and live their lives according to how they see fit. Expressives wonder at this behavior because it is not as harmonizing as how the Expressive lives. At its essence, this relationship grouping boils down to the Expressive wanting a deeper connection with the Trailblazer. Expressives want to feel they are intensely loved and cared for. Don't we all? But for the Expressive, living this way is non-negotiable. When they do not feel this deep connection, they wonder if the Trailblazer truly cares for them. Expressives have an everlasting desire that manifests itself more acutely when around thinkers like Assertives and Trailblazers. Expressives are operating from their hearts, not their heads. It is important to note that this desire is for an ideal, and it can only be truly fulfilled in a relationship with God. Expressives have an intense ability to connect on a deep level, but not everyone can do this, so the Expressive is sometimes let down. Trailblazers, who at times can seem detached (especially the more introverted ones), can help in this relationship pairing by speaking more about their inner feelings, conveying much care, and regularly showing up to do relationship work which demonstrates to the Expressive how much they love them.

Trailblazers and other Trailblazers

It is a unique pairing in a relationship set to have two people assessed into the same personality profile, in this case Trailblazer and Trailblazer. One has to probe a little deeper about communication between the exact same types. First off, you are likely to feel a strong connection with each other based upon your fundamental similarities: a dynamic mind always percolating with new ideas, a yearning for independence, and a desire to cut to the chase and discuss real issues without being afraid of what others think. Both of you are abstract, utilitarian, and influencers which means you might look past what's right in front of you, and the here and now, to mine new possibilities and horizons that have not been considered or tried before. You will relish the fact that you can have lively discussions without fear of hurting the other's feelings. Your conversations will center on impressions, ideas, and theories. You will love not getting bogged down in the details of day-to-day conversations; just the facts ma'am, unless you are speaking of something important where the details are critical. You both like to play practical jokes and no doubt will use your mischievousness to constantly prank or surprise each other.

One value you both have is your pursuit of truth and justice. You both appreciate the value of fairness, and using logic and reason you will strive to find out how a decision someone has made can be just. One thing to look out for is arguing for the sake of arguing. There is a tendency for Trailblazers to pick a fight when none exists; this can be doubly true for a Trailblazer Trailblazer pairing. Also, remember to compliment each other and say thank you for small acts of kindness. Though a compliment isn't necessary, it is sure nice to hear once in a while to feel appreciated for all the hard work one does. Each Trailblazer tends to trust their own reasoning and believe in your ability to come to the correct conclusion about issues. There is a tendency to overuse logic and analyses when sometimes you just need to fully listen to what the other is saying. Therefore, listen fully and completely to each other. It is important to remember that listening is a gift to be given daily, not just on someone's birthday or at Christmas. When one is sharing, do not simply plan out the next thing to say but give the gift of true listening. Both of you are levelheaded and do not get especially hurt when one of your beliefs is challenged. However, since both of you are likely to operate more from your head than your heart, it is important to take time to develop the emotional side of life together. Talk about your inner feelings once in a while and hurts you may have or have had. Try to go deeper in demonstrating compassion and empathy for each other. Life is more than perfunctory tasks and accomplishing your goals each day. Trailblazers will thrive with a little romance once in a while. Take delight in buying flowers or gifts for each other and creating intimate interactions. It can be fun to partake in areas outside of the normal functioning.

So, what will your pairing, and nearly every other pairing, argue about? The little things like driving habits, the temperature in the room, and which music, movies, and television shows are the best. The other items that can cause friction in any pairing are the details in life like who will pay the bills, mannerisms, messiness, and how one may go about day-to-day chores. When one Trailblazer does criticize the other Trailblazer, it often comes across as super direct and forceful. An extra note here, it is incredibly important for a Trailblazer to feel respected. Everyone likes to be respected, but for Trailblazers it is a balm for their soul. They crave competency and part and parcel to being competent is being recognized as such. If you honor each other and continue to provide common courtesies, your relationship will stand the test of time. As with all types there will be bumps in the road and some stress until you learn about which things are most important to each other, which items you will leave alone, and which items are hills to die on. Speaking of stress, when Trailblazers are under heavy stress, they become increasingly domineering, refuse to admit failure, and are repetitive to no end. A fellow Trailblazer can use directness and call them out on it. Communicate often and keep the fires burning. With regular gardening of the relationship, your partner will be your home base, supporting you for a lifetime.

Expressives and other Expressives

It is a unique pairing in a relationship set to have two people assessed into the same personality profile, in this case Expressive and Expressive. One has to probe a little deeper about communication between the exact same types. First off, you are likely to feel a strong connection with each other based upon your fundamental similarities: the desire to feel significant, to deepen relationships, and to always be passionate in your pursuits. Both of you love to connect with people and go deeper in communications, so the chance of you having a shallow relationship is nonexistent. You are both sensitive, thoughtful, and idealistic. These will serve you well in having a deep connection with one another. It is important in any relationship not to take each other for granted, and this is especially true for this relationship pairing. Remember to compliment each other and say thank you for small acts of kindness. Though a compliment isn't necessary, it is sure nice to hear once in a while to feel appreciated for all the hard work one does. You will find each other interesting and stimulating to talk to. What is important to an Expressive is to feel like you have opened up to them and they feel they know you. In this pairing that will happen regularly. You both have a deep concern for other people and want to make a positive dent in the world to help others. Your desire is to change the world one person at a time and make it a happier, more caring, and gentler place. News of violence, school shootings, and wars seem to tangibly wound your soul. Your desire is for others to succeed and be happy. Empathy and listening are strengths in this pairing, but I will write this anyway—listen fully and completely to each other. It is important to remember that listening is a gift to be given daily, not just on someone's birthday or at Christmas. When one is sharing, do not simply plan out the next thing to say but give the gift of true listening.

Of note with this authentic type, Expressives do not easily hide from others how they are doing or how they feel about you. If an Expressive's countenance is off, this is the check engine light on for their soul, and it needs to be taken seriously. So, what will your pairing, and nearly every other pairing, argue about? The little things like driving habits, the temperature in the room, and which music, movies, and television shows are the best. The other items that can cause friction in any pairing are the details in life like who will pay the bills, mannerisms, messiness, and how one may go about day-to-day chores. When one Expressive does criticize their partner, the receiving end Expressive is likely to take the blow extremely personally. There can be some stress until you learn about which things are most important to each other, which items you will leave alone, and which items are hills to die on. Speaking of stress, when Expressives are under heavy stress they become increasingly sullen with a "woe is me" attitude. When angry with another Expressive, they may exhibit an "I'll get even" attitude which is dangerous. A fellow Expressive can use calm and interpersonal skills to gently call them out on it. Communicate often and keep the fires burning. With regular gardening of the relationship, your partner will be your home base, supporting you for a lifetime.

10

A CHAPTER FOR LEADERS TO CREATE EFFECTIVE TEAMS AND HANDLE CONFLICT

Personality profiles help organizations develop teamwork and reveal workers' strengths and weaknesses in order to get the mission accomplished. Depending on what type of work is getting done, there might be a necessity to have the right people, in the right place, and at the right time. For instance, if I was in a laboratory, I might predominately search for the Trailblazer type. If I was in a military unit, needing special forces personnel for a tough mission, I would search for Assertive personalities. If I worked at a nonprofit with lots of people interaction, I would want the Expressive type to be part of it. However, this book is purposely not a vocational guidebook. There are many other books which aid people on who to hire.

My purpose in writing this book, and this very chapter, is to allow people of different personalities to find a rhythm, a groove in which to work together without getting on each other's nerves. Is it possible to put a Trailblazer and a Loyalist together, or an Assertive and an Energizer? Absolutely! If they have read their profiles, are aware of their own strengths and blind spots, and are willing to grow in self-awareness, then there is a great chance of success.

There are many aspects to the makeup of our personality.

The important thing in relationships is to be yourself and not wear a mask. It is okay to have emotions, and it is okay to feel detached sometimes. Be who you are, freely; and then, as needed, reflect on your strengths and accept your weaknesses in order to make significant improvements which can help you get along better with others.

A repeating theme in this study is to remember that others are not out to get you or annoy you. They do things differently. They say things more severely or negatively than you may think appropriate. Every opportunity of annoyance is also an intersection whereby you can experience reflection and growth. You don't have to try to change the way others feel, just let them feel it. Perhaps there are things we need to change about ourselves to get along better with others. Be open to that.

People are flawed, but there are no flawed personality types. There are also no perfect personality types. They are what they are. We are wired a certain way, and some aspects we can't escape, but we should never use our type as an excuse. Our profiles can help us evaluate why we think a certain way, and how we respond in certain situations, but we are in no way bound to negative behavior. And no one can be, or should be, put into a box. People change. Our personalities morph over time with an increase in self-awareness. We can always be better, and we should strive for that.

CREATE EFFECTIVE TEAMS

The clarion call for leaders is to know the people on their teams. To make the team more effective at the mission, leaders must know with what personality types they are working. Once everyone on the team has taken the online diagnostic, the leader will be able to gain great insight into how to effectively manage their team by the material in the rest of this chapter. The following is a graphic which shows a snap-shot demonstrating what each type can contribute to teamwork.

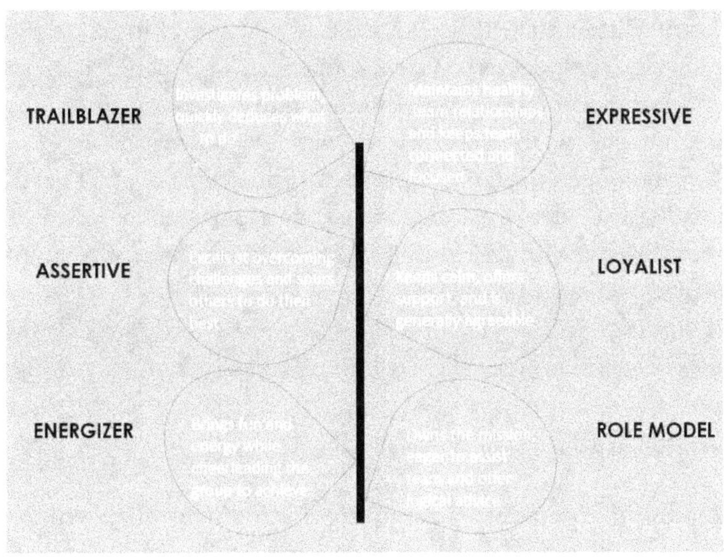

The following paragraphs provide information on how each type contributes toward teamwork, and also can take away from it. Remember, being aware of a predisposition you might have can empower you to change unhealthy behavior and reinforce positive behavior.

ROLE MODEL

Team Enhancements: Role Models are goal-oriented and bring a high motivation for the team to succeed. But what is important is that they don't let their motivation to succeed interfere with how they treat people. Role Models are responsible and typically high producing. They can be counted on when the going gets tough because they have an intangible desire to succeed and accomplish their goals.

Team Distractors: Role Models can have an overfocus on the rules and desire everyone to cooperate. This could lead to creating guilt or stifling the more carefree team members like the Energizers and Trailblazers who are utilitarian and less socially cooperative. Also, instead of approaching conflict head-on, Role Models have a tendency to avoid conflict and not squarely deal with relationship matters, which can lead to more problems down the road.

ENERGIZER

Team Enhancements: Energizers bring focus for what needs to be accomplished on a project, along with having a good grip on reality. No matter what happens, these buoyant people often keep a great attitude, even during trials and hardship—unless they are unfairly attacked. Another positive is that Energizers possess an abundance of energy, which can make stressful situations more fun for everyone.

Team Distractors: Energizers need to be aware they can stretch the patience of those around them with too much cheerfulness. Just because the Energizer is bouncing around and happy does not mean everyone else is having a good day. Also, if they are too joyful in a stressful situation, they can appear superficial or scattered to more serious team members.

<u>LOYALIST</u>

Team Enhancements: Loyalists are usually supportive, pleasant, and dependable team players who are easy for others to be around. They adhere to rules and schedules and possess a quiet congeniality that usually isn't an affront to anyone. As long as there is no conflict within the team, Loyalists can be counted on to contribute heavily to the project.

Team Distractors: Loyalists can be taken advantage of and become a catch-all for others' complaints. What this means is that the Loyalist will hesitate to tell people the truth. They also don't really want to listen to the other teammates' problems; but they would rather suffer silently and allow the person to vent. Eventually this will bog down the Loyalist. Also, Loyalists can become paralyzed by team conflict, and when the bullets start to fly, they can shut down, becoming too stressed to see the big picture and contribute.

<u>ASSERTIVE</u>

Team Enhancements: Assertives are usually assured, confident, and glad to contribute or take charge to get things accomplished. They respect authority and rules and can get their team organized and onto the right path. Their no-nonsense approach to the mission is refreshing for most of the types and others will willingly follow the Assertive because of their confidence.

Team Distractors: Assertives can be too competitive and make the task more important than the team. When this happens, people can feel "run over" by the Assertive. Assertives can also become impatient, overbearing, and quick to criticize others, yet slow to speak praise. Eventually this corrodes all of the good will that might have been established earlier and work against the altruistic goals started by the Assertive.

TRAILBLAZER

Team Enhancements: Trailblazers typically bring what is called visionary leadership; this is the ability to live on the edge of the future and conceptualize the mission in new terms, with all of its risks, and see possibilities everywhere. Trailblazers, with their strong utilitarian, decision-making nature, can assist a team to cut through red tape. They are usually not bothered by deadlines and procedures while finding creative solutions.

Team Distractors: Trailblazers can become so consumed with reaching higher goals, they miss important milestones. They are usually not satisfied until their vision for the project is fulfilled. Trailblazers can also become impatient with the current progress and argue for the sake of arguing, which tests everyone's patience. They can even appear arrogant if tasks become mundane, which will annoy other team members simply trying to get through their day.

EXPRESSIVES

Team Enhancements: Expressives possess high interpersonal awareness which enhances decision-making. They often know how teammates are doing without being told. They can somehow pick up on clues regarding teammates' feelings usually missed by other types. Much like Energizers, Expressives are also enthusiastic, spontaneous, and courteous team members who thrive in group activities.

Team Distractors: Expressives can get feelings muffed by others and exhibit mood swings. Comments that might bounce off an Assertive or Trailblazer might impact an Expressive deeply. This usual "fly by the seat of their pants" type can become restless with delays and can even cause divisiveness with their bickering. Also, they sometimes struggle with follow-through.

Here are some easy-to-read summaries of what was just explained:

ROLE MODEL

Team Enhancements:
1. Goal-oriented with motivation to succeed, but not at the cost of relationships.

2. They are responsible and high-producing; can be counted on in tough situations.

Team Distractors:
1. An overfocus on rules can create guilt in more carefree members of team.

2. Find it easier to avoid conflict than to approach it head on which can lead to greater problems later.

ENERGIZER

Team Enhancements:
1. Possess a good grip on reality and keep a great attitude despite trials and hardship.

2. Possess an abundance of energy and make situations more fun for everyone.

Team Distractors:
1. Can stretch the patience of those around them with too much cheerfulness.

2. Can appear superficial or scattered to more serious team members.

LOYALIST

Team Enhancements:
1. A supportive, pleasant, and dependable team player.

2. They adhere to rules and schedules and possess a quiet congeniality that usually isn't an affront to anyone.

Team Distractors:
1. Can be taken advantage of and become a catch-all for others' complaints.

2. Can become paralyzed by team conflict and too stressed to see the big picture and contribute.

ASSERTIVE	TRAILBLAZER	EXPRESSIVE
Team Enhancements:	Team Enhancements:	Team Enhancements:
1. Assured, confident, and glad to contribute or take charge to get things accomplished.	1. Visionary leadership with ability to see possibilities everywhere.	1. High interpersonal awareness which enhances decision making.
2. They respect authority and rules; can get the team organized and on the right path.	2. Can help team cut through red tape; not bothered by deadlines and procedures while finding creative solutions.	2. Enthusiastic, spontaneous, and courteous team members who thrive with group activities.
Team Distractors:	Team Distractors:	Team Distractors:
1. Can be too competitive with the task becoming more important than the team.	1. Can become consumed with reaching higher goals and not satisfied until their vision is fulfilled.	1. Can get feelings muffed and exhibit mood swings.
2. Can become impatient, overbearing, and quick to criticize, yet slow to speak praise.	2. Can become impatient with current progress and appear arrogant if tasks become mundane.	2. This usual "fly by seat of pants" type can become restless with delays; can cause divisiveness with their bickering.

HANDLING CONFLICT

Occasionally, people on teams have a hard time seeing eye-to-eye and will look at things differently to the point of interpersonal conflict. In that case, it is important for leaders to communicate several things: first, remind them that the individuals are on the same team and have shared goals; second, that it doesn't help the situation to create a scene, make things awkward, or to embarrass someone; and third, a time-out in order to de-escalate a situation can be very beneficial when things get too heated. All six personality types have a unique way they encounter conflict, and the following charts can be useful to a leader in learning how each team member might respond when triggered.

EXECUTIVES DEALING WITH CONFLICT

Role Model: These harmony-loving people are no fans of conflict and will work hard to avoid it. They are perfectly capable of standing up for themselves and will not hesitate to stand up for a friend or loved one if they feel that person is being unjustly persecuted. When under stress, Role Models often utilize the blame game, pointing a finger at someone else for the problems or conflict.

Loyalist: They typically avoid conflict at all costs but as unresolved issues build up, they can be known to be a teapot, spilling out over everyone present. Sometimes the Loyalist will utilize the silent treatment, punishing the other person for a perceived offense. Overall, Loyalists dislike making others angry and will try in various ways to keep things calm, even giving a false sense of assurance, such as "We're all still friends, right?" which usually increases other's angst.

Assertive: These usually calm people do not like it when other people bring foolish drama into their lives, but Assertives will definitely stand up for themselves when needed. Rather than avoid conflict at all costs like Loyalists, Assertives will readily enter into the fray because they enjoy taking control of situations. And they will shut down a confrontation if it is not going their way. Like Role Models, Assertives will also utilize the blame game, calling out other people for their lack of attentiveness to things.

<u>EXPLORERS DEALING WITH CONFLICT</u>

Energizer: They do not like conflict and will avoid it at all costs. An Energizer's main goal is to have fun, and conflict disrupts their ability to enjoy life. During conflict, Energizers typically try to ignore that it is happening at first, hoping it will go away. When that doesn't work and they are forced to face it, emotions like anger, and then tears, might spill out because, like a Loyalist, they are a little bit like a teapot.

Trailblazer: Bring it on. Nothing stimulates a Trailblazer more than a healthy discussion of ideas where two people can speak with candor. They can sometimes be seen as *wanting* conflict or *taking pleasure* in conflict because by nature they are the most argumentative type. Robust discussions are how Trailblazers feel they learn, and how they manage friendships. They want to learn from others. It is also how they feel they can educate others on their ideas. Last note, Trailblazers can sometimes snap on people who are bothering them.

Expressive: They do not like conflict so will pick their battles carefully. Expressives do not want to burn bridges in future relationship growth and will go to great lengths to be as diplomatic as possible in hopes everyone can be heard and not hurt. They are not pushovers and can stand up for themselves, but they do not like discord in the relationship, so they will avoid an argument if at all possible.

Explorer Loyalist: They do not mind conflict as long as people are expressing themselves in healthy and calm ways. Explorer Loyalists want to be allowed to state their opinion, but they will not tolerate someone who is out of control and yelling at them. Explorer Loyalists have sensitive hearts and they will shut down if someone is being unnecessarily cruel.

The aim of this section on teamwork and conflict is to benefit leaders who wish to create a more synergistic work environment. It is the true challenge of every leader to know how to motivate their team members, not only to accomplish the mission, but to get along with their colleagues. The material in this chapter can be a helpful enabler for team members to have a greater awareness regarding the strengths and weaknesses for everyone on the team. The goal is for any group of people to develop into a more cohesive, collaborative, and affirming team.

11

THE "BIG 5" AND THE Z FACTOR

THE "BIG 5"

As I mentioned in the opening chapter, academia types hold firmly to the theory of the "Big 5" personality traits: Openness, Conscientiousness, Extraversion, Agreeableness, and Neuroticism. This section will define these categories and measure them against the *RELATE* personality model. Of note, these five areas operate on a spectrum of low to high within every personality type. The bar graph below is merely a snapshot of the averages associated with each type, but they can vary quite a bit depending on outside factors and on a person's level of humility and character.

Openness is one of the easier concepts to explain. A person who has this trait is willing to try new things, creative, imaginative, and receptive. These people are usually more abstract in their thinking and possess high levels of curiosity. Essentially, they show receptivity to new ideas and experiences. People low in openness are a little more dogmatic and closed off. Explorers are generally higher than Executives in the openness category, but it is not always true and depends on the person.

Conscientiousness means a person is more detail-oriented, persistent, driven, dutiful, and deliberate. A person who has this trait is usually seen as competent, organized, and possessing self-discipline. People low in conscientiousness seem more flexible and easygoing, and in their worst form more unorganized or lackadaisical. Executives are generally higher than Explorers in the conscientiousness category, except for the Trailblazer type who strives for competence and is more detail-oriented than the other two Explorers: the Energizers and Expressives.

Extraversion is defined by those having more warmth, positive emotions, and excitement seeking. These people are very social, they start conversations, and they don't mind being the center of attention. People who are low in extraversion are more reflective and reserved and would not be described as jovial. What Energizers and Expressives might lack in conscientiousness, they make up for in extraversion and are the highest two types in the *RELATE* model. The Loyalist type usually has the lowest extraversion score. Also, some Assertives and Trailblazers function as more introverted than extroverted.

Agreeableness is associated with people who are cooperative, care about others, and are more compliant than most. People high in agreeableness are usually genuinely interested in other people, are kindhearted, and possess empathy. Those low in agreeableness are usually seen as competitive and argumentative. The Role Model, Energizer, and Loyalist types have the highest degree of agreeableness, and the Trailblazer type is typically on the lower end of the scale.

Neuroticism is the one "Big 5" trait most hard to navigate. The other traits all seem to have a more positive side to them, but no one wants to be known as neurotic. However, it is one of the keys to understanding the way people behave and it is necessary to include it in this study. People with neuroticism possess feelings described as emotionally reactive and excitable. In its more mature form, it is seen in people who have anxiety, anger, depression, or simply get upset easier than most. It is a gauge for how likely a person is to interpret events as threatening or difficult. Simply put, neurotics fret about things more than others and can appear insecure. Those who are low in neuroticism are seen as resilient, calm, confident, and emotionally stable. Low neuroticism people manage their stress well and are slow to anger. Looking for a silver lining, there is a potential upside to mild neuroticism in that it can enhance self-reflection and creativity. But when this develops into constant cynicism and self-loathing is when it becomes destructive.

In the *RELATE* model, the Role Model, Energizer, and Loyalist types have a greater propensity to lean toward neuroticism than the other three types. This seems to stem from their high level of agreeableness and desire to be liked. People in these three types might overthink things they have said to others and wonder how their words were received. When they are feeling insecure, they have a hard time being themselves, and the insecurity usually stems from wanting to be liked by other people and please people. However, as seen in the chart below, all six types are materially low in neuroticism, and the truly neurotic stems from factors outside of the *RELATE* lens of personality typology. Here are three observations regarding neuroticism:

1. Non-neurotic people tend to gravitate toward other non-neurotic people in an effort to minimize what they consider unnecessary drama.
2. The truly neurotic cannot tolerate being around others like themselves; so, because of number one above, they can feel separated from others and lonely.
3. When neurotics do tolerate each other, it is only for brief periods, to enable their misery to feed off each other.

Here is a chart Illustrating *RELATE* to the "Big 5":

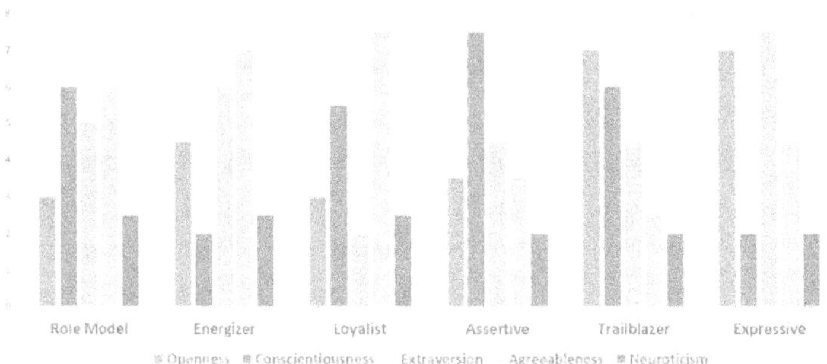

Z FACTOR PEOPLE

The Expressive type and Explorer Loyalist type possess a trait in common that no word or phrase can adequately describe, so I call it the Z factor because it is a summation of multiple parts. The Z factor essentially means the individual has a mixture of being an abstract thinker, socially cooperative, and individualistic all in one person that creates a synergistic effect to how they see the world and go about their daily lives. They are also the two most idealistic personality types in the *RELATE* ensemble. I discussed, in previous chapters, the difference between concrete thinkers and abstract thinkers and the difference between being socially cooperative and utilitarian, but I will break it down in detail in the next few paragraphs, then summarize what the Z factor means.

To be a **concrete thinker** is to focus on the physical world around you and to take things literally. No one is totally concrete, and everyone is on a spectrum in how their thinking works. Concrete thinkers tend to take things at face value and are very literal with their words and ideas. They do not read into things too much nor coordinate data to come up with alternative, or imaginary meanings. Children can be imaginative, but they are typically more concrete in their thinking, believing what they see and trusting the words they hear.

To be an **abstract thinker** means to have the ability to consider concepts beyond what is observed physically. Abstract thinkers have the ability to recognize patterns, analyze ideas, and synthesize data in a way that is often missed by concrete thinkers, not that one is better than the others. Oftentimes abstract thinkers can miss obvious items seemingly right in front of them. Abstract thinkers are consumed with the bigger picture, which is why the Trailblazer, Explorer Loyalist, and Expressive—all three abstract thinkers—are comingled in the Explorer camp. They look for, and live in, the deeper meanings of things. They quickly make cross-disciplinary associations and are comfortable living in the gray and creating metaphors for life. They will talk about what something or someone is becoming, and they can see life as an intense drama. Energizers are the exceptional Explorer in that they are more concrete in their thinking, though they love big picture ideas.

The difference between being **socially cooperative** and utilitarian is that to be socially cooperative one has to like adhering to societies' prescribed methods of functioning. It feels as if you are on one giant team that needs to work together to accomplish a common purpose or benefit. Socially cooperative people respect rules and guidelines and try to make things easier on others. In the opposite corner are utilitarian people, who are not so much seeing a common operating picture of how everyone should act. **Utilitarian** people operate with a positive attitude toward those things that are productive and efficient and possess a negative attitude toward those things that are ineffective and useless. They do not like wasting time on societal niceties and typically choose the decision that brings the greatest dividends. One small example, if a socially cooperative person had limited time to clean their vehicle, they would start with the outside. A utilitarian individual would prioritize cleaning the inside first because they are not as concerned with what other people think as much as what makes sense to them; being able to enjoy a clean and comfortable ride. Don't read too much into this small example, it is simply a quick illustration of how decisions might be made.

If you consider the analogy of ends, ways, and means, **utilitarian** people are more concerned about the ends and are willing to streamline the ways and means to achieve the best end. If it can be done better or faster, utilitarians are all for it. It is the consequences of the actions that matter, not so much the actions themselves. Utilitarians crave maximum benefits. Socially cooperative people are equally concerned about both the ends and the ways. Their more balanced approach will not sacrifice good relations or good standing to achieve a better end. Carefully consider these next words—there is no moral gradient within the six personality types; the socially cooperative personality types are wanting the entire system to win, and the utilitarian is less preoccupied with the system, especially when they cannot see the gain for the system. Of the six types, all but the Energizer and Trailblazer types are socially cooperative. This does not mean the two utilitarian types are selfish and the other four types are others-focused; remember—no moral gradient. The Energizers and Trailblazers have the capacity for incredible self-sacrifice and giving, along with selfishness; and the socially cooperative types equally have the capacity for other-centeredness or self-centeredness. The narcissist chapter at the end of this book will highlight what is most concerning when studying behavioral flaws. Now, back to the Z factor.

Z factor people are also **individualistic,** so how does that settle up with being socially cooperative? To be individualistic, in this case, does not mean to work against the group and go it alone or be self-reliant. On the contrary, the Expressive type and the Explorer Loyalist type love people and want to interact with them. In the sense I am using the word *individualistic* is that Z factor people are unique and have individualism. They like to feel genuine and original, and to some, they might come across as peculiar or idiosyncratic. But it is really important for Z factor personality types to be themselves and not sheep. These people are true originals and really give seasoning to the stew of personalities.

So, let's put all of this together. The Z factor means to be an abstract thinker, socially cooperative, and individualistic. In the *RELATE* model, only the Expressive and the Explorer Loyalist types fall into this camp. These are incredibly idealistic and intuitive people who see life in patterns or perhaps as one big drama. They search out the deeper meaning of events and care about values and ideals. They are usually authentic, one-of-a-kind people who are very cognizant about how they are living and participating in this world. They are creative people who look for silver linings and seek out harmonious relationships. They dislike conflict, as everyone should, but they don't mind bringing conflict into a situation to bring healing and redemption. They have no problem asking hard questions and calling out others if they are not doing the right thing. This is their idealism kicking in—*people should be who they say they are and not be fake!* They abhor social injustices and are empathetic to others. They like to be known as "mercy motivated" and enjoy helping other people navigate their feelings.

Z factor personalities feel as if they are experiencing a deeper part of life than others, but desire to share what they have, so others can experience it as well. All personality types can feel they have a high calling and purpose in life, but Z factor types sense their calling and purpose more acutely. Forming deep connections with others is a part of this, and it means the world to them when they are allowed to help others grow. If you look at the eight traits of these people, it will summarize what was just described. They are Comprehending, Unsystematic, Contemplative, Unconventional, Perceptive, Connecting, Idealistic, and Passionate.

In summary, there is not one type more special than the other types. They are all different and have unique contributing factors to their personas. But certain types align with each other. The Expressive type and the Explorer Loyalist type share the Z factor mentioned above. The Energizer type and the Trailblazer type are utilitarian in nature, while the Role Model, Loyalist, Assertive, and Expressive types are socially cooperative. The Explorer Loyalist, Trailblazer, and Expressive types are abstract thinkers, while the Role Model, Energizer, Executive Loyalist, and Assertive types are concrete thinkers. Also, the Role Model type and the Assertive type have a meticulous bent to them, which means they can be extremely careful and precise. It also means that they are very careful with details. When an Explorer type is explaining something, Explorers need to use facts, documentation, and patience to get Role Models and Assertives to agree to their plans. The Loyalist types and Expressives have a merciful bent to them which is expressed by being generous, kindhearted and compassionate to others. Also, the Role Models and the Loyalists are the most harmonizing, meaning they are friendly and agreeable, wanting to make sure people are not offended. Last, the Assertive type and the Trailblazer type predominately use their head (thinking) when making decisions while the other types use their gut (instinct or feeling). Here is a summary breaking down the concepts in this section:

Z factor: Expressive and Explorer Loyalist
Utilitarian: Energizer and Trailblazer
Socially cooperative: Role Model, Loyalist, Assertive, and Expressive
Abstract thinkers: Explorer Loyalist, Trailblazer, and Expressive

Concrete thinkers: Role Model, Energizer, Executive Loyalist, and Assertive
Meticulous: Role Model and Assertive
Merciful: Loyalist and Expressive
Harmonizing: Role Model and Loyalist
Lead with thinking: Assertive and Trailblazer
Lead with instinct: Role Model, Energizer, Loyalist, and Expressive

Now on to the hard but important topic of narcissism.

12

KEY FACTORS OF NARCISSISM AND HUMILITY

This book assumes its readers will use the material to grow in self-awareness. However, its aim is not to make people consumed with self. It is one thing to read a book to understand about differences in personality and another thing to be blinded by pride and self-absorption—the definition of narcissism. Self-awareness is not just comprehending how you come across to others. It is understanding how your words and actions are impacting others and how others are receiving you and your output. Over time we should grow in these things. It is helpful to comprehend how people receive us, yet this is where some have a blind spot.

Narcissistic people have a world view that revolves around self and how to manage self and promote self. Since they have a persistent need for admiration and a lack of empathy, they have little interest in helping others advance causes that do not directly help the narcissist. It is imperative for the narcissistic person to be seen in a positive light, at all times. And, consequentially, this often means putting others down. No matter who they are with, the conversation gravitates toward critiquing other people, because in the narcissistic mind, to create permanent damage to others lowers others and elevates self. Narcissistic people have very little regard for what other people think about issues. The narcissist wants to get their views across, and their points to be told and retold, receiving admiration in the process. The only time the narcissist cares about what others think or say is when it involves them and when they are presented in a positive light. Otherwise, they have no use for the information.

Is it possible for any human to live in a world like this, where all they ever think or care about is themselves and their own reputation? Absolutely. These people exist all around us (albeit, hopefully in low numbers). They are not bad people; they have simply given in to temptations others somehow resist. They allow themselves to believe only the good press and none of the bad. They allow themselves to think that they have one of the only noble hearts. They allow themselves to think that most other people cannot appreciate them for who they really are, and that others are out to get them. They have given in to the temptation of one of the first lies in humanity—that others are withholding good things from them and they need to reach out and take the good for themselves. That the nourishment of self is the highest good, not loving God and others. This brings us to the blind spot.

The blind spot is the inability to truly put yourself in another person's shoes and empathize with them. The narcissist goes through life either not considering, or not caring, about the viewpoints and struggles of their neighbor. There is always a negative reason in the narcissist's mind as to why someone is struggling; they did not work hard enough, they were not smart enough, or, the greatest sin of all, they didn't listen to me enough! Their mirror is their altar. In a way, they worship themselves. And speaking of mirrors, when a narcissist looks into their rearview mirror, they cannot see the people behind them they have run over and belittled as real people with valid struggles. Only the narcissist has had to struggle. Only the narcissist has had to overcome unfair obstacles. Other people are only useful in what they can do for the narcissist. The narcissist will only be happy with people who can give them an advantage, or make them look better. The narcissist is drawn to and blinded by the greatness of their own resplendent light. And it blinds them to the real needs of others.

This is more than being self-assured, it is being too sure of self. A normal, emotionally healthy person who is self-aware can have a vigorous self-assurance if they are competent in their task. We can like the skills we have been given as long as it doesn't lead to admiring ourselves or seeking for others to admire us.

The healthy, self-aware individual doesn't use others' compliments to fuel their ego. The healthy, self-aware individual does

not let the good press they hear about themselves interfere with their work and demand for the good press to grow by encouraging others to read it. Self-aware people know they have done ten things right and ten things wrong in trying to get to their position in life. They understand that when they receive unfair criticism, they have also received unfair praise. They know that when someone attacks them for something, the accusation might have some truth to it. They level things out in their minds and resist the temptation to become prideful when others give praise, nor become resentful when others give scorn. And last, self-aware people know that sometimes people they disagree with are elevated or rewarded, and that is okay; they do not have to demonize these people to others. These attributes of emotional health described in this paragraph is how you define humility.

The narcissist does not have these basic skills. Their ability to resist the temptation to fight back is broken, so they wage war. Their ability to resist the temptation to think they are better than others is broken, so their ego grows. In both these areas, they possess a certain amount of fragility and are not able to stand trials without a good bit of martyrdom. And at times, a narcissist will pick a fight with someone just because they are bored. Self-absorption always leads to a discouraged heart and a desire for others to feel worse.

How did they get this way? At some point in their lives, they stopped allowing negative feedback to have any validity. They decided they were better than what anyone else might think of them. They decided that they were the only ones who knew the real truth of the situation, that they are special, the best, and deserve recognition, respect, and praise. Psychologists think that a portion of this behavior is influenced by the narcissist's childhood, that they either received too much praise, or the opposite—not enough acknowledgement. Whatever the case, it is grievous what narcissists inflict on themselves and others.

I'm writing this to encourage you to not be like these people. Be the self-aware individual who can take both praise and criticism in stride. Study the blind spots in your personality chapter, and be open and honest with people about them. This type of meek behavior, instead of turning people away from you, may endear you to them. It is rare to find a person comfortable enough with themselves not to hide their faults. People usually don't judge you for who you truly are, people judge you for who you pretend to be.

I realize there is risk in writing a book like this where it can be used to tear others down in the false belief there are some personality types better than others. But, as I've mentioned before, there is not one type that is better than any other type. Each of the six types, as unique and special as they are, are part of the grand mosaic of humanity God wrought forth since the beginning of human history.

The goal for each personality type is to embrace humility. At its essence, humility means not to think of yourself as better than others. It does not mean to berate oneself or overly criticize your own shortfalls. It means having a realistic view of who you are, and seeing your strengths and weaknesses as a whole. Humility is an indispensable virtue for friendship in every culture known to man. No one wants a friend who thinks they are superior. No one wants to be bullied or to be one-upped after they tell a story. People enjoy spending time with others who are eager to listen, yet not afraid to provide candor when warranted. When both admiration and admonitions are reciprocated in healthy ways, both given and received for what they are, that is entering into the world of true friendship. There is no fear in love.

Alas, all of us are on the narcissistic spectrum. To be a self is ipso facto to be self-ish. However, life is about how we control that bent, and to the degree that we inject humility into our thinking, our conversations, and our everyday lives. To be low on the spectrum means to have a healthy acceptance that our lives are not the center of the universe. To be high on the spectrum means to have a life as outlined in the paragraphs at the beginning of this chapter. As seen on the chart below, we are all somewhere on the line, and depending on the day, we may be more or less narcissistic with our words and actions. The goal is to increase our humility. For information on sociopathic behavior see the Endnotes.

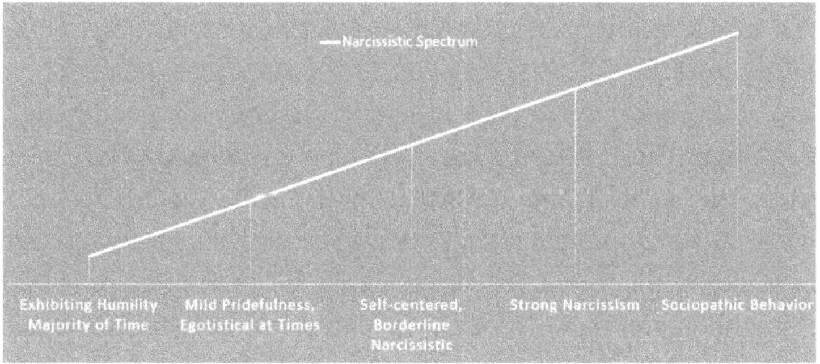

Here are some of the key points on humility mentioned above:

1. **A humble person doesn't garner other's compliments to fuel their ego.**
2. **A humble person doesn't let the good press they hear about themselves influence them.**
3. **A humble person knows their life is a mixture of victories and failures.**
4. **A humble person understands when they receive unfair criticism, they have also received unfair praise.**
5. **A humble person knows that when someone attacks them for something, they consider how the accusation might have some truth to it.**
6. **A humble person is not outraged when those they do not get along with are rewarded or promoted.**
7. **A humble person knows that just because they disagree with someone, it is not a reason to demonize them to others.**

For some, it may be hard to define humility or know exactly how it should look in their own circumstances, but everyone knows when it is missing. Also, no one is fooled when a narcissist feigns humility by playing the victim and putting themselves down in order to bait people to compliment them. When you still think you are dealing with a reasonable human being, you might think you can persuade a narcissist to take the high road. But your magnanimous behavior will typically be met with either a rebuke or passive aggressive silent treatment. Nothing bothers a narcissist more than being accused of something they are actually doing. It infuriates a narcissist when someone else can see them for who they are. Therefore, boundaries are essential.

Yet, to be fair, and to bring humility into this discussion, we don't always initially understand why someone acts the way they do; they may have struggles we cannot see. It is important to give others the benefit of the doubt before slapping a negative label on them. Even truly good people have some flaws, and deeply flawed people have some good things about them; sometimes it takes time to see, but it is true.

The inventory below is a short summary of the points of this chapter and can be helpful criteria to see more clearly with whom you are dealing:

Is a person a narcissist?

1. Does the person acknowledge how their words and actions impact others?
2. Does the person have the ability to promote others and not themselves?
3. Does the person have the ability to truly care for the needs of others?
4. Is the person content with not being the center of attention?
5. Does the person have the ability to listen to constructive feedback patiently, without lashing out?
6. Does the person have the ability to speak well of others and is not constantly critical of those not in the room?
7. Does the person have the ability to put themselves into another's shoes and express empathy for those less fortunate?
8. Does the person often complain of unfair obstacles?
9. Does the person have a hard time being accountable for their own behavior?

10. Does the person seem self-absorbed, like it is only their world that matters?
11. Does the person believe they are unique or of high status, and they should only spend their time with others in that category?
12. Does the person seem fragile?
13. Does the person feel as if good things are being withheld from them?
14. Does the person often switch clubs or groups because others are less smart, or just don't get them?

For the truly narcissistic personality type, questions one through seven would have an answer of "no" and questions eight through fourteen would have an answer of "yes." Note, no one will be a perfect narcissist; there may be a few questions that don't apply to them.

The following is a contrast of Narcissistic behavior vs. Humility *(the goal!):*

Narcissism	**Humility**
1. Lack of empathy	1. Concerned for others
2. Boastful	2. Nonchalant about achievements
3. Superiority	3. At ease with self and others
4. Monopolizes conversation	4. Patiently waits to speak
5. Overbearing at times	5. Energizes others
6. Easily offended	6. Takes criticisms in stride
7. Sense of martyrdom or taken advantage of	7. Feels blessed beyond what they deserve
8. Routinely criticizes others	8. Routinely speaks well of others
9. Preoccupation/too much awareness of self	9. Not worried on how people perceive them
10. Feels unloved by others, uses it as a tool	10. Rarely conveys low-esteem feelings
11. Uses people to advance their own cause	11. Serves other people

A final admonition—avoid narcissistic people at all costs or you may quickly find yourself alienating those who truly love you, and aligning yourself with those who don't care for you. If you have to be around narcissistic people, use healthy boundaries by limiting time with them, calling them out on their behavior, and not being swayed by them when they are buttering you up for something because you may just be their next meal.

"It's a deep and all but certain truth about narcissistic personalities that to meet them is to love them, but to know them well is to find them unbearable. Confidence quickly curdles into arrogance; smarts turn to smugness, charm turns to smarm."

-Jeffrey Kluger

13

WHEN IT ALL FALLS APART

Sometimes relationships can implode, even with our best efforts and intentions. How do people move on with their lives when there is a rupture in an important relationship? This chapter focuses on an area that is hard for some people to grasp, that of letting go of the wrongs done to us, and releasing other people from what we believe they owe us. It is natural to write about this after a chapter on narcissism, but perhaps unnatural in the confines of a personality book. The intent here is that since this book is about nourishing healthy relationships, I must also address when there is an impasse and there is a difficulty that cannot be worked through. It is hard when the other person does not acknowledge the break or their role in destroying a relationship. So, what do you do in these tough circumstances?

There is no magic wand to heal broken relationships. However, I know that it is possible to forgive other people when they don't acknowledge any wrongdoing, or even when they are holding a grudge against you. For me personally, the motivation for this kind of action is anchored in my faith. But knowing I am writing to a larger audience I want to provide several important reasons why forgiveness should be given.

To forgive another is to grasp your larger self; not the self that requires coddling, but the self that aspires toward goodness and benevolence. Unfortunately, forgiveness in modern counseling is encouraged chiefly so that one can sleep better at night, like taking Ambien or Nyquil. I've heard a "non-forgiver" described as someone who takes a poison pill hoping someone else will die. What bothers me about these ideas is how they arc back to nourishing the self and are presumably suggested so that the self continues to thrive. But God does not forgive so He can sleep better at night. I've spent my entire adult life teaching that forgiveness is not meant to be self-nourishing; it is performed as an act of giving, and sacrifice, both of which are root elements of love.

No one is perfect, and people are not able to undo what they have done to us, even after they have a change of heart and regret their actions terribly. There are stories of Nazi concentration camp guards who sought out forgiveness from those released from the camps after the war; a request which seems unimaginable. Yet to not forgive a person is to keep them permanently in their worse state. And the reversal of this is also true; in the eyes of others, I am kept permanently in my worse state. I am inspired by the story of Corrie ten Boom, prisoner 66730 from Ravensbruck during WWII, who was asked to forgive her captor and realized it was a task impossible for her, but not for God. Though she could not find the words or actions to embrace the man, she felt compelled to do it anyway.

I like some of the thoughts of philosopher Hannah Arendt on forgiveness; when she described life as being unpredictable in both actions and reactions. To provide a quick snapshot, she estimated that just as evil things in our life cannot be predicted (or we would try to avoid them), the act of forgiveness can never be predicted. It acts in an unexpected way, and it destroys that in-between part of life which relates us to, and separates us from, others.

She also intimates in this thought about life being unpredictable—that to live in a world of unforgiveness is to make life an instant fossil record, with each imperfect action instantly ossifying us into a failed promise of personhood. Without being forgiven and released from the consequences of what we have done, our capacity to act would, as it were, be confined to one single deed from which we could never recover.

I desperately need forgiveness for my selfish actions, whether done intentionally or unintentionally, and so does everyone else. To refuse others our forgiveness hardens others and us. To forgive others keeps us human, and a conduit of the love of God.

Going back to aspirations (from the third paragraph of this chapter), I suppose there could be a rare individual out there who wants to remain a mediocre person. However, I can't help to believe that nearly everyone else wants to go into that in-between part of life and improve humanity. Someone told me once, "But you don't know how bad they hurt me!" Yet forgiveness is a bridge to the life we aspire to. If we determine ourselves to be loving people (which is a high aspiration), what follows is to release others when we are unexpectedly injured. A caution here; what I am writing about is not self-help as an act of sheer will. It is more.

There is more to this life than meets the eye. We humans did not evolve to the point of forgiveness; forgiveness is fracking into a hidden reservoir, a power, a love, a fountain; always available, never diminished, and strong enough to set every captive free. Again, Corrie will be our guide:

On the day Corrie ten Boom embraced the German guard and offered him her forgiveness, she wrote the following in her journal that evening: It is not on our forgiveness any more than on our goodness that the world's healing hinges, but on God's. When he tells us to love our enemies, he gives, along with the command, the love itself.

(14)

THE MISSING INGREDIENT

What does success in life look like for you?

Some people might answer the above question with being rich, having a beautiful spouse, or being powerful. What if I asked how do you define life success? Would your answer change? I think life success has a more permanent feel to it. The following is a story about how two people visualized life success for themselves.

There was once a businessman, on an island vacation, walking the beach one afternoon. He encountered a fisherman resting his back against a palm tree, with a straw hat pulled over his eyes. The extroverted businessman initiated a conversation with the man and asked him what he does.

The fisherman edged up his hat so he could see the stranger speaking to him. "I fish from my canoe for a few hours in the morning and catch two or three large fish. I sell them at a local market, and then take a long siesta on the beach, watching the waves roll in, and dozing sometimes," he said with a twinkle in his eyes.

The businessman was flummoxed, "Why don't you stay out all day and catch many large fish?"

"Because I make enough money to support my family, and

besides, I like going out in the bay in the morning when it's cool, but then enjoy resting here on the beach when the sun is hot."

"Well don't you see," replied the businessman, "If you caught more fish, then you could buy a better boat, and maybe hire some workers to help you."

"What would that gain me?" asked the fisherman.

"Well, then you could make even more money, and perhaps buy another boat or two and hire more workers," explained the businessman.

"And then what?"

"Well then the sky is the limit," the businessman proudly proclaimed, thinking of his MBA and accomplishments back on the mainland. "You could own a fleet of ships, buy your own cannery to eliminate the middleman, and maybe even franchise out. You could have your headquarters in New York City or Los Angeles. You could become a wealthy man. Doesn't that sound nice?"

"But what would be the result?" asked the fisherman.

"Don't you see?" asked the businessman, as if it was obvious. "Then you could retire early and do whatever you want, spending your life traveling to places like this beach village to enjoy the sun," he explained eagerly, as if completely justifying his argument.

"That's exactly what I'm doing now," the happy fisherman replied, winking at the man and nodding good day before pulling his straw hat back over his eyes.

The bewildered businessman walked away slowly, pondering why any man would waste his life away.

I have four observations to make from this story. First off, each person's definition of success is different. For the businessman, he can think of no better way of being happy than pursuing a bigger and better lifestyle. For the fisherman, he was happy with the life he was living. He enjoyed fishing while it was cool in the morning and resting when it was hot. He may or may not enjoy supervising other workers to fish, or for that matter, running a business enterprise. In this story, two cultures collide.

A second point is that it is important to have goals, but what if you don't achieve them; will you cease to be happy? What if the fisherman sacrificed and pursued the businessman's dream but found that it wasn't as easy as it had been packaged in their conversation? It is always important to enjoy the journey, while keeping an eye on the destination. Are you energized by your life pursuits? The fisherman was content to spend a few hours in the water and the rest of the day on the beach. This was his daily routine, vacation, and life fulfillment.

A third consideration is that not all of us can pursue a simple life on a beach catching a few fish, even if we wanted to. There can be competing demands in our lives that keep us from what might look like a life of ease. Perhaps medical obligations or extended family care create extra monetary needs. However, we can learn from this story that the ingredients of happiness and contentment can, in one way, be as graspable as a mental change, to focus on what really matters, and where we want to end up, not on what other people desire of us. Are there people in your life pushing you into decisions that you do not want? Perhaps they are trying to accomplish their own goals through you. What is it that you want in life? How do you want to get there?

A final point—and I would call this the missing ingredient of many life stories—it is not enough to do something important with your life. For multiple reasons an overarching quest for importance might potentially lead to disappointments, such as burn out or family neglect. What's missing in the story is that it does not address making your life one of lasting importance, and that means investing it for the greater good of mankind. Every soul not only has a divine spark but a divine purpose. Being successful in life is not enough; discovering your sacred calling is what will energize you and those around you for the rest of your lives. The words "sacred calling" means that it is connected with God and God's path for your life. If you do not yet have a sense of what this might be, simply saying yes to God, to the small things he may be asking you to do, can be a start.

Part of this goes back to figuring out what kind of person you want to be (genuine, strong, faithful, etc.), which is vaster than your personality type. Instead of starting with goals, take a step back and ask who you want to be. Do you want to live a life characterized by serving others and leading by example? Do you want to be a person who delivers on your promises and commitments? Being the right kind of person—someone you can be proud of when you are in your later years—must be preeminent to the discussion of life success and is an underlying message in this book. How do you want to be remembered? What thoughts do you want in your children or grandchildren's minds as they walk out of your memorial service?

In a final analysis, I am not suggesting living your life in a way to please other people, or to make them think you are great. What matters most in relationships are unselfish investments in other people. Loving them. To come alongside others—not with an agenda for them or advice for them—but showing warmth to people for who they are, encouraging them, learning from them, caring for them, and investing in them. This is why I wrote this book, to help people value and love other people.

So, what is the first step? Start with self-honesty and respect. Do you respect yourself enough to enter into the process of healthy change?

Life is sacred.
You are valuable.
You deserve respect.
You are worthy of love,
and you are capable of loving others deeply.

Your time matters.
Your words matter.
Your deeds matter.
You matter.
Seize the day, and live like there's no tomorrow.

ENDNOTES

1. Part of the research of this study involved testing 300 participants over the course of eighteen months. There were batches from different sectors/sizes of society. These batches included students, military members, married couples, a church, a small group, etc. Most of the rest were individuals—people from different age groups, religions, nationalities, and regions of the world with which I had access. I collected an even number of male and female participants and discovered some unique trends in the results. For instance, the Executive family is composed of 58% females and 42% males. The Explorer family is composed of 42% females and 58% males. When looking at specific types, the Executive Loyalist type had the largest divergence between the sexes of 70% female and 30% male. Ironically, the Explorer Loyalist sub-type had the closest correlation between the sexes with 48% female and 52% male.

2. Harvard study on Positive Relationships. *Good Genes are Nice, but Joy is Better.* Liz Mineo, April 11, 2017, *Harvard Gazette,* *https://news.harvard.edu/gazette/story/2017/04/over-nearly-80-years-harvard-study-has-been-showing-how-to-live-a-healthy-and-happy-life*

3. *U.S. Teen Girls Experiencing Increased Sadness and Violence.* Centers for Disease Control and Prevention, 2/13/2023. *https://www.cdc.gov/media/releases/2023/p0213-yrbs.html*

4. Executives vs. Explorers.

Use of power. For Executives, they are unique from Explorers in how they utilize power. Executives see power as belonging to institutions, so power is delegated to individuals based on status. Executives are more authoritarian with their power than Explorers. If the lieutenant does not follow the orders of the captain, then the lieutenant should be reprimanded. In contrast, Explorers do not see issues in blacks and whites. Power is authority, but it is also relational. For instance, an Explorer might argue that since the captain did not communicate his orders clearly, or at the right time, then the actions of the lieutenant should be given more review. There is a little more of a conditional nature to situations of power with Explorers. For them, life is a little grayer. Yet for the Executives, even asking the question about how the captain communicated the order is an affront to the system. *Why question this?* Executives may ask. The lieutenant was obviously wrong because of his rank.

Handling difficulty. What is the difference in how these two groups handle difficulty? Usually, there is a head-on nature with Executives; the sooner you get the unpleasantness over with the better. It is important to bring the issue to the table and deal with it, so it doesn't get worse. Explorers, on the other hand, tend to negotiate heavily when there is a difficulty. *Perhaps not everything has been taken into account. Have you considered this scenario?* Explorers ponder situational factors repeatedly, sometimes belaboring even fine points. Executives don't care for this and call it weaseling because it is a time waster. If someone is wrong, they should be confronted and punished quickly, then everything can go back to running smoothly once again. There are exceptions to this, which will be brought up within each personality. For instance, Loyalists, though a member of the Executive family, do not like to bring up conflict; and Trailblazers, though they are members of the Explorer family, delight in difficult conversations.

Processing data. Another distinguishing category is processing data. For Executives, there is a practical nature by which to look at the world. For instance, besides all the good in the world, it also includes pain, suffering and disappointments, which should be factored in. There is usually no free lunch, and people who are too friendly are suspect. Explorers might see this attitude as pessimistic, but Executives take offense to that and consider themselves the premiere realists of the world. As for Explorers, they tend to have an idealistic view of things and rarely focus on negative possible outcomes. Explorers might be called by Executives as pie in the sky dreamers, but Explorers prefer to be known as optimists who hope for the best. Explorers might ask, "Why borrow tomorrow's troubles?" If something failed in the past, that doesn't mean it will fail now. Whereas for Executives, the past is the best predictor of the future. As you can see, both viewpoints have validity to them.

5. The "Big 5" Personality Traits. There are many sources to this information but one from a Psychology Today article is: *https:// www.psychologytoday.com/us/basics/big-5-personality-traits*

6. Sociopathic behavior. This is a term used for people who exhibit anti-social personality disorder. These are individuals characterized by having an impaired sense of empathy and remorse, and it is easy for them to ignore or break social norms. They can lie, cheat, deceive, steal, or stalk others without guilt. Sometimes a sociopath's evil actions can be shrewdly premeditated.

7. Corrie ten Boom story. Charles Causey, *The Lion and the Lamb: The True Holocaust Story of a Powerful Nazi Leader and a Dutch Resistance Worker*, Bloomington: Westbow Press, 2016.

8. Hannah Arendt, *The Human Condition (2nd Edition)*, Chicago: University of Chicago Press, 1998.

9. The Happy Islander story. This is a version of a popular story usually entitled *The Fisherman and the Businessman*. Online sources reference Heinrich Boll's short story *The Mexican Fisherman* as the source.

FOUR SESSION STUDY GUIDE

Session #1 Questions

1. What personality type are you?
2. When looking at your personality chapter, what are the accurate descriptions about you? What are the things that do not seem quite as accurate?
3. Do you think you are a blend of a couple of types? Explain to the group what two types you are.
4. In your own words, describe the difference between the Executives and the Explorers (see Chapter One and the Endnotes for more information). Which one are you? Give examples of how you see this play out in your life.
5. When looking at the four lead traits and the twenty-two personality traits for your type, are all of these really close, or are there some that are a stretch? Share with the group the ones in which you gravitate to the strongest.

Session #2 Questions

1. What animal type are you? Is this a good description of who you really are?
2. When you have friends or family take the *RELATE* personality assessment do they fall into your expected categories, or are there some surprises?
3. Under your type, when it discusses how you respond under a great amount of stress, please give an example of how this may or may not be true of you.
4. In Chapter Nine the author addresses how each type gets along with other types. Are these paragraphs helpful to you as you navigate relationships with other types? What else might be helpful to know when entering into new relationships with people?
5. In Chapter Ten the author discusses how each personality type works within a team structure. Please give an example on how this is valuable to leaders based on your own type, or for those who you lead.

Session #3 Questions

1. In Chapter Ten the author discusses how each type handles difficulty. Did you find this information accurate for your type? Why or why not?
2. In Chapter Eleven the author introduces a summary of the "Big 5" personality traits. Are the levels of the five traits approximately true for you and your personality type?
3. In your own words, please describe to the group what neuroticism means. Have you encountered a

neurotic person? If so, please explain to the group some of the traits exhibited by this person.

4. In Chapter Eleven the author discusses the Z factor. In your own words, please describe to the group what the Z factor is.

5. Is there anyone in the group who is part of the Explorer Loyalist or Expressive personality type? If so, have them explain what the Z factor means to them.

Session #4 Questions

1. In Chapter Twelve the author gives an explanation regarding narcissism and its impacts on relationships. Do you know a narcissist? Without giving names, try to describe the person to others.

2. In your opinion, what is at the root cause of narcissism? How do you combat against it when you see it in others? How do you combat against it when you see it in yourself? Where are you at on the narcissistic spectrum?

3. What is the author's definition of humility? Do you agree that humility should be the goal for every personality type? Why or why not? Is it possible to be humble even if you are not inherently a humble person?

4. What are some ways the author suggests that forgiveness is important? Is forgiveness something you struggle with in your own life? Please explain. Is it possible to forgive someone even if they do not acknowledge any wrongdoing?

5. What are your goals in life? Do you have a plan to get there? What are the potential major roadblocks to you accomplishing your goals? In your own

words, what is a sacred calling? Do you know what yours is?

ACKNOWLEDGMENTS

This book is the expression of thousands of conversations for nearly half a century. If I were to address the full measure of those who helped in its conclusions, I would list nearly every one I have ever known. I won't bore you with that. At the beginning I was blessed with amazing parents. Calvin Gerald Causey and Patricia Jean Causey, you did right by me. Thank you for your freely given love; even when I exhibited adolescent pride and exuberance you were ever patient. I was also blessed with an amazing set of siblings; Calvin, Carol, and Nathanael, you've brought such a depth to my life; not only as siblings, but as three of my closest friends who I admire. You mean so much to me. This book is not lightly dedicated to you, *RELATE* is wrought because of you; you have always been there for me and taught me important life lessons. Thank you, dear ones.

My greatest blessing is my immediate family. My wife Lauri and four children, Nickolas, Madison, Hannah, and Isaiah, were usually my first guinea pigs when developing assessments and different models to view personality. It started early in our marriage. Lauri and I were given a personality assessment. It helped us understand each other more as individuals, and that we were doing and saying things, not with the intent to pick a fight, but because we were programmed that way. Lauri is the love of my life and she has such a uniqueness in personality—I could never find another like her in a thousand years. I love to love her. My children and their spouses have taught me much about life and are a large part of what brings meaning to projects like this one. My prayer is for them not to be afraid.

May you shine in love, humility, honesty, and self-awareness—the virtues of courage. Occupy your space, be who you truly are, let others see you.

I can never thank enough my editor, Vicki Zimmer, who has worked on my books faithfully since I started writing. Thank you again, Vicki. Thank you for all the edits, and thank you more importantly for your friendship, support, and partnering with me on projects like this one. Vicki, along with her husband Mark, are always the first to volunteer to help with new material, whether being beta readers or spending hundreds of hours on meticulous line edits. I wish I could repay them adequately for all they have done for me and my family. Mere words don't seem to cut it, but here they are—you're the best, thank you!

A hearty thank you to all of my beta readers and content advisors: Brady, Gabe, Mallory, Sharon, Thomas, Mark, Tony and Karen, Garret, Kiana, and Sarah. Your feedback, suggestions, and questions were extremely helpful in putting the finishing touches on this material. Another set of eyes is always good, and having you part of my team gave extreme encouragement. Rich and Karen Auer, thank you for your contributions, friendship, and encouragement throughout this project. And, my partner in ministry Tony, I hope to be leading events with you when we return from overseas.

I've written enough books to know that the message will not get out to others without a magnificent launch team. Though I do not know your names at the time this book had to go to press, thank you for helping me to launch this book! I also thank my early endorsements of *RELATE*: Cynthia, Mark, Quintin, and Tony, how generous you are. Again, much thanks from the heart. It truly takes a large, dynamic team to publish a book like this. I thank my publisher Dave Sheets, along with my agent Bob Hostetler and the Steve Laube Literary Agency. And last, the myriad of participants who took the *RELATE* assessment as it was in development the last few years. Your kindness overwhelms me. Thank you. The above contributions were given with a dream of helping many future readers in their relationships. We, as torches, are to let our lights shine, and those named above are resplendent.